Don't pick up this book if you're looking for a comfortable read. Every page contains a story or a challenge that will make you uncomfortable. Every chapter prods and pushes Christians to reevaluate their priorities, reexamine their faith, and redirect their lives to the crying needs in our world that only Christ can meet. You will tell the stories from this book in your sermons and lessons. You will use the challenges in this book to move Christians around you to a no-holds-barred discipleship, and in the process you will be moved out of your own comfort zones into extreme expressions of your faith in Jesus. All this will happen as you discover that you agree with the author's conclusion: anything short of extreme Christianity may not be Christianity at all.

—Mark Taylor
Editor and Publisher, *Christian Standard*

In an era when Muslim extremists are beheading innocent people to advance their cause, Dr Ajai Lall and his son-in-law Josh Howard challenge believers to die to self to advance the cause of Christ. Using moving, contemporary examples of Christ-like courage and martyrdom, this book throws down the gauntlet to lukewarm believers to embrace a bold faith that takes up a cross and follows Jesus. A much-needed message for this desperate time.

—Bob Russell
Founder of Bob Russell Ministries
Author of *Acts of God* and *When God Builds a Church*

The Bible is full of men and women who paid with their lives because of their love for JESUS and His church. Unfortunately, our churches aren't. That's the challenge issued by Dr. Ajai Lall and Josh Howard in this excellent new book. Many of those, whose stories you'll read in this book, I've met and heard their testimonies as I fought back tears, embarrassed that our commitment to JESUS and His church in America wouldn't come anywhere close to theirs. Ajai Lall is a modern day Apostle Paul. Josh is his enthusiastic, passionate modern day Timothy. When you see the magnitude of their ministry, what they're accomplishing for the kingdom, you'll feel like you're living the Book of Acts all over again.

—Barry Cameron
Pastor of Crossroads Christian Church in Grand Prairie, TX and
bestselling author of *The ABC's of Financial Freedom*

Christian Extremism: A Life Worth Dying For portrays God's extreme love and sacrifice for us through compelling stories and strong challenges. If you're looking for a book that will challenge you to do great things for God, this is the book. Ajai Lall and Josh Howard make a strong case for living an extreme life and a life you will not regret.

—Dave Ferguson
Lead Pastor—Community Christian Church,
Lead Visionary—NewThing
Author of *Exponential* and *Finding Your Way Back to God*

You definitely want to get a copy of this book which will take your commitment to live the gospel and share the gospel to a whole new level!

—Dave Kraft
Leadership Coach and Author of
Leaders Who Last and *Mistakes Leaders Make*

It's hard to both paint a huge vision for what God could do and fill in the blanks along the way with very practical next steps. This book does both. You will be challenged, encouraged, and maybe even have your toes stepped on a little bit. But Ajai and Josh will help you see your role in God's plan to change the world.

—Kyle Idleman
Best-selling Author of *Not a Fan*

So often Christians are lumped in with extremists of different faiths and unfortunately many who say they follow Jesus don't understand what that means. This book clarifies what it means to be a Christian extremist and gives us real living examples of it. As one who has been to India to see what Ajai and Josh (As well as the whole CICM team) are doing, and meet the people they are writing about, I can tell you that they have the unique right to speak on this subject. It's not just theory and philosophy for them, they live in the reality of the consequences. They are giving their lives away and give us a model to follow. As they live as Christian extremists, they are making a difference and show us how to make one too. It's an honor to endorse this book because these people live for Jesus.

—Jim Putman
Sr. Pastor Real Life Ministries,
Author of *Disciple-Shift* and *Real-Life Discipleship*

Some books are like a flute, light and playful, while others are a lone violin, soulful and reflective. But this book is a trumpet blast! These words rouse our half-asleep faith and call us to charge headlong into the spiritual battle. Brothers Ajai and Josh are living courageously on the kingdom frontlines, and as they wove together stories of Biblical heroes and some modern-day faith heroes they know, I was inspired. But I was also challenged to honestly examine my own heart. If you want to take seriously words like "deny yourself" and "take up your cross" and "follow me," this book will show you how.

—Matt Proctor
President of Ozark Christian College

Ajai Lall and Josh Howard have written to all of us about the real life stories of what is happening in India. I have made three trips to India over the last 8 years and heard many of these testimonies personally. They are real and something people around the world need to know. Many of us have no idea how hard it is to be a Christian in an Extremist world. We need to pray for these people on the front lines every day. Thank you Ajai and Josh for your book and what it will mean to many people around the world.

—Doug Crozier
CEO of The Solomon Foundation

CHRISTIAN EXTREMISM

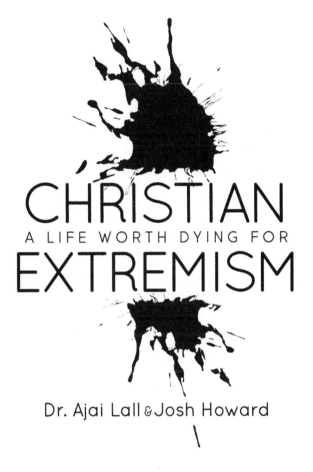

CHRISTIAN
A LIFE WORTH DYING FOR
EXTREMISM

Dr. Ajai Lall & Josh Howard

HIGHERLIFE
PUBLISHING & MARKETING, INC.

Oviedo, Florida

ISBN: 978-0-9907578-5-6 Paperback

Published by HigherLife Development Services, Inc.
HigherLife Development Services, Inc.
100 Alexandria Blvd. Suite 9
Oviedo, Florida 32765
www.ahigherlife.com

Printed in the United States of America.

Dedication

This book is dedicated to all of the Christian extremists across the world today. To those who are risking their lives every day for the sake of the Kingdom. You are our heroes. The world is truly not worthy of you.

Table of Contents

Introduction

O VER THE YEARS, an army has been rising up in our world, an army that marches on its knees. Instead of using bombs and guns to win their victories, this army fights with love, grace, and forgiveness. Their members live among us. They look and dress like the average person who lives next door, yet they live a completely different lifestyle from the mainstream—a lifestyle that is not about them but about others. They live as soldier-servants of the Most High and are daily sacrificing their lives for the sake of the kingdom of God.

Unfortunately, there is another army rising up as well—an army that is spreading hate and destruction. This is an army that would steal, kill, and destroy rather than give, resurrect, and restore—an army of darkness.

Then there are those who live somewhere in the middle. These are people who have not yet chosen a side. They live lukewarm,

1

content, and easy-going. They are the army of Laodicea who have not chosen the narrow path of extreme living on either side, but are trying desperately to hold on to the hope that comfort, security, and safety in this world is possible.

This book is about the first army. By telling their stories and lifting them up to be seen, it is our hope that you will be inspired to join their ranks, or be encouraged and emboldened if you already count yourself a member.

Or perhaps you consider yourself a member of that massive middle group. It is our passionate prayer that this book will awaken within you a hope, a hunger for something more—that living lukewarm, striving for comfort, and security would somehow lose its appeal. May you be awakened to the potential to live with unbridled passion, purpose, joy, and significance that only comes from joining the ranks of the extreme love-based life of the army of light.

Are you willing to believe God wants something more from you—has something more for you?

May we no longer be content to sit idle while the world is being left in darkness. The title of this book may shock you, but keep reading. Jesus wants to bless you with both the hunger and ability to live an extreme life. He wants you to proudly march along side your brothers and sisters as a member of that first army— an army of Christ-followers, disciples, and world changers. An army of Christian extremists who are living a life worth dying for.

The question is not whether we will be extremists, but what kind of extremists we will be.

—MARTIN LUTHER KING, JR.

The Positive Kind of Extremism

E LIVE IN a world that is full of extremism. Every time you turn on the television, you see another extremist group that has done something horrible. Islamic extremists were to blame for the attack on America in 2001. ISIS has been responsible for countless attacks in Syria, Iraq, and many other countries across the world. Hindu extremists were to blame for the attack on Christians in 2008 in Orissa, India. Hundreds of churches were burned down, and thousands of Christians were killed or displaced. To this day, there are still Christians who cannot return to their homes.

I met with one of the victims from Orissa recently and heard her gut-wrenching story. Her husband was a pastor who was faithfully preaching about Jesus in their Indian village. God was using him in wonderful ways. When persecution broke out, the extremists went after the pastors first.

Before the woman's eyes, they beat her husband to death and then cut his body into pieces. They forced her to watch the entire time. She was holding her newborn baby in her arms. After they were through with her husband, they grabbed the baby and hurled the child against the wall of their home, killing her instantly. Then they grabbed the woman, raped her over and over again, poured kerosene on her body, and tried to burn her alive.

Extreme hate met extreme faithfulness.

They left her there on fire.

By the grace of God, the fire went out, and she survived.

As she was sharing her story with me, I could not imagine what that must have been like; the trauma she experienced was incomprehensible. She looked me in the eye and said, "Here's what I would like to tell Christians all across the world: if I can stay faithful to Jesus after such a horrific event, why can't you?"

Amazing. Extreme hate met extreme faithfulness.

6

But extremism isn't always negative. We have also had extremists throughout history who have made wonderful changes in our world. Here are some examples:

- Martin Luther King, Jr., led an "extremist" group back in the 1950s and '60s to transform an entire nation. His extreme commitment changed America and the rest of the world.

- It was an "extremist" group that fought against Nazi Germany in France.

- It was an "extremist" group that launched the Boston Tea Party and helped to establish an entirely new nation that would become a world superpower.

- Mahatma Gandhi led an "extremist" group to completely destroy British rule in India and to gain independence for one billion people.

- Nelson Mandela led an "extremist" group in South Africa, which led to the destruction of apartheid in the entire country.

You see, extremism isn't inherently good or bad. God can use it to create wonderful things in the world, and the enemy can use it to bring destruction. The extremism we are calling you to in this book is different from what we've seen in recent months. It's something much greater.

This kind of extremism will not result in destroying lives or burning buildings or hurting people. Instead, it will result in a move of God that can transform this world in an incredible way—not through anger, bombs, and pain but through love, commitment, and sacrifice.

Throughout the course of this book, we are going to look at the different qualities of a Christian extremist. Qualities like extreme love, forgiveness, and sacrifice. You will read stories of people from all over the world who are living out these qualities on a daily basis. Our prayer for each of you is that you will be inspired to action—that you will take on each quality and live it out every moment of your life.

We invite you to experience a new move of God. We invite you to become a Christian extremist.

> The only way to change this world for the better is to use the principles of extremism in a positive way.

Do you realize that hate is much easier to feel than love? Pain is much easier to offer someone than forgiveness. Quitting is much easier than staying faithful. Blowing something up is much easier than rebuilding something that is broken. If we are truly going to fight the evil in this world, we must step up and be intentional about it.

It won't happen accidentally. The only way to change this world for the better is to use the principles of extremism in a positive way. If the world continues as it is, business as usual, it will just continue to get worse. We need people who will stand up and live an extreme life. We need people who will love instead of hate, build instead of burn, sacrifice instead of take, and stand in the face of difficulty. We need men and women who will live the life Jesus has called us to live—a life filled with love, peace, joy, grace, and forgiveness.

We need Christian extremists.

What drives us? Where does this extremism come from? It's the love of Jesus that compels us, just like it did Paul! And Jesus' love is amazing, right? Here is a story about how amazing His love and grace truly is.

Azad Khan was associated with a group of criminals and thieves. They killed people, stole their belongings, and did not feel a bit of guilt afterward. Azad was the kind of guy people would steer clear of when he approached them on the street. The entire city feared him. He was in and out of prison more than fifteen times, but each time he was bailed out by "high-up" rich people who would hire him to do their dirty work.

One night, he committed a crime and was on the run. The police had been tipped off, and they were chasing him through the city on foot. As he was running, he saw a church building, and he ran inside to hide. He was hoping the police didn't see him. As he stepped inside, he saw that the place was full of people. He thought, *This is great. They'll never find me in here!* As he sat down in the back of the church, a man stepped up on stage and began to preach. Azad had never heard about the real Jesus before, but God was about to change that. The man who was preaching started talking about Jesus on the cross. His sermon was about the two thieves who were crucified next to Jesus.

Think about that for a second. Isn't God amazing? Here was a true thief, sitting in the back of a church, and the preacher's sermon was about the thief on the cross. You can't make stuff like this up. Only God can do this. Think about how much time in advance God planned this. He planned it through the preacher's preparation time. He planned it through the police tipoff. He planned it through the time of the church service.

Everything was in place. The Master Christian Extremist was at work, and His eyes were on an extremist at a whole different level. As Azad sat there and listened, his heart began to open to what the preacher was saying. The pastor said, "Both thieves had done horrible things. That's why they were hanging on those crosses. But one thief pleaded for forgiveness, and the other thief mocked Jesus until his last breath. One thief died without hope, and the other thief died with the promise of

Jesus: 'Today, you will be with me in paradise.' The question is: which thief are you?"

And who was the preacher delivering the sermon that night? My father, Dr. Vijay Lall.

I was just a kid, but I remember, night after night, Azad coming to our home to learn more about this Jesus whom he had heard about that night. I was scared to death. My brother, David, and I would peek through the crack in our door to make sure this criminal wasn't harming our dad. We didn't like him coming around late at night, but my father didn't mind. He was a Christian extremist, too, and he loved Azad and wanted the best for him.

After a few months, Azad accepted Christ. The Master Extremist's grace had transformed the criminal extremist's hard heart. Over the following years, Azad went to Bible college and devoted his life to ministry. Eventually, he began to travel from prison to prison sharing his testimony with the prisoners. Since then, Azad has preached to more than four hundred thousand prisoners, and God has used him to bring thousands of them to the feet of Christ.

This is what happens when people live out extreme love. They are transformed and that, in turn, transforms many more people. This is the love that compels us, the love of God that transforms the hardest of hearts. With a love like that behind us, what can possibly stop us?

Here's what I know: it's *great* to read stories like this. It's inspirational and powerful. But don't you ever get tired of reading about other people's experiences? Don't you want to experience them for yourself? Don't you want to live them out and be *in* the story? It's time to get off the sidelines and into the game!

Will you step up and join the ranks of the Christian extremists who have stood firm in their faith, living their lives as a shining beacon for those who have lost their way? This call to God's service does not mean you have to quit your job and move your family to Africa to become a missionary. It does not mean you have to become a pastor, live among the homeless, or donate all of your money to an orphanage. But... God may be calling some of you to do these things.

In general, this call is simply for you to follow Jesus' example right where you are, doing what you do best, to help people around you who are looking for a better way to live. When others see your unwavering obedience to God and the joy and peace that result from it, they will be drawn to you, and that will be your opportunity to reach out to them, in a way no one else can, and share God's message of hope.

In Romans 12:6–8, Paul says, "We have different gifts, according to the grace given us. If a man's gift is prophesying, let him use it in proportion to his faith. If it is serving, let him serve; if it is teaching, let him teach; if it is encouraging, let him encourage; if it is contributing to the needs of others, let him give generously; if it is leadership, let him govern diligently; if it is showing mercy, let him do it cheerfully."

Maybe you are a teacher who can reach out to a child who is growing up in an oppressive home. Maybe you are a supervisor with an employee who needs guidance about a substance-abuse issue or a family crisis. Maybe you work in a nursing home and see elderly patients struggling to come to terms with their salvation as they breathe their last. God has planted you right where He needs you to reach certain people. You never know when someone is watching you, wondering how they can experience the same joy and confidence in the future as you do. So be extreme in your obedience, your commitment, your love, your forgiveness, your prayer, your boldness, your generosity, and your sacrifice. We will talk about each one of these hallmarks of the Christian faith in upcoming chapters.

Are you ready for the challenge? It won't be easy, but it will definitely be worth it. If you're willing, let's begin.

*God has a habit of picking
up nobodies and making
them somebodies.*

—TIMOTHY KELLER

*One ordinary man or woman
connected to an extraordinary
God can make a difference.*

—PAM FARRELL

Chapter

You Can Do This!

KNOW WHAT YOU may be thinking: *I can't do this. This just isn't for me. I'm not like these extreme Christian leaders. I don't have what it takes.*

> "If God is with me, then what else do I need?"

Here's the deal: if God is with you, what else do you need? Let me write that again. This time, say it out loud to yourself.

"If God is with me, then what else do I need?"

And that is the point. All we need to do is agree with a God who has a passionate, incredible agenda for the restoration and reconciliation of people—all people everywhere. Christianity is full of living testimonies to the inherent power of our Lord.

Pastor Jagdeesh was born in an incredibly poor family in the middle of India. His father was a shepherd and made very little money. The family often went to bed hungry because there wasn't enough food for them. Because of their poverty, Jagdeesh was not able to go to high school.

"I never understood why I was in this situation. I felt hunger constantly, and I wasn't able to go to school with the other children," he recalled later.

As Jagdeesh grew older, a man in his village shared the Gospel with him, and he became a Christian.

"After becoming a Christian, my views began to change. Instead of worrying so much about my situation, I started to look around me and see the hurt and pain of others," he said. "I prayed that God would give me an opportunity to help people who grew up like I did."

It was out of this heart that Jagdeesh and his wife started a children's home in a severely impoverished village of India. Although he had little education, Jagdeesh had a heart for Jesus and a passion to serve children. Today, they are taking care of fifty-two children who were orphaned by their families. He may have been uneducated, but God was with him, and that's all he truly needed.

We all receive burdens from the Lord through the Holy Spirit. What are the things that move your heart with the compassion of Christ? What do you see right now that breaks the heart of God? Consider how God can use you to impact these areas for His Kingdom. Making a list might help. As a matter of fact, stop reading and make a list right now. The book will be here when you get back. List all of the areas that God has placed on your heart that break His heart, and make that list with no holds barred. Don't think about your limitations; focus on His abilities through you. Somewhere on that paper is an area God wishes to transform through you. Take courage!

When they saw the courage of Peter and John and real-ized that they were unschooled, ordinary men, they were astonished, and they took note that these men had been with Jesus.

—ACTS 4:13

"They took note that these men had been with Jesus." That's the key. A passionate relationship with Jesus is the real issue here. Not education or being an awesome leader or being adequately equipped.

It's about Jesus.

You can have educated men and women who have no passion for Jesus whatsoever, and you can have uneducated men and women who have passion for Jesus.

Here's the question: do *you* love Jesus?

Seriously.

Truly.

Your willingness is all He needs.

Do you deeply love Him? Are you faithful to Him? Are you willing to obey Him, no matter what comes your way? If the answer is yes, then that's all you need. Your connection to Jesus is the most vital part of your life. Under His supervision, you simply "do the good things he planned for us long ago" (Ephesians 2:10 NLT). On your own, you can do nothing worthwhile or lasting, but if you love Jesus, you are His, and His desire is set upon you. You are no longer on your own. He is directing you. He can effectively minister through you, planting your feet on the path He has chosen. Your willingness is all He needs.

You can do this. Really.

Who did Jesus use to turn the world upside down? Think about it. Fishermen. Tax collectors. Some educated, some not so educated. He looked for open hearts.

You may be thinking, *How can I be a Christian extremist? You talk about all these amazing stories of people doing incredible things, but how can I do something like that? I'm not very educated.* Or maybe you're thinking, *I didn't go to Bible college* or *I'm nothing special.*

One of my favorite stories in the Bible is when Jesus stepped off a boat and walked on the land, meeting different people. That's when He met a demon-possessed man. This guy was crazy. Nobody wanted him around. They even tried to keep him chained up in a graveyard! He was the guy people warned their children about. High school students dared each other to go mess with the crazy, naked guy. The villagers had kicked him out. His family had rejected him. Since they didn't want him around, they put him outside town as an outcast.

But then Jesus showed up and treated him like a human being. Like a child of God. *Because he was.* Jesus could have gone to anybody, but he went to this man. He looked him in the eyes, and He began to talk to him. Then He cast out the demons, and He healed him completely—mind, body, and soul. Jesus approached the man who nobody wanted around and healed him and loved him in a way nobody else ever had.

That's our Jesus. That's the Jesus we're following. Now watch what happens next.

The demon-possessed man was in his right mind again. His life had been healed. He sat at the feet of Jesus and began to learn from Him. As he learned, Jesus turned around and began to walk away. As Jesus stepped back into the boat, the formerly demon-possessed man said, "Wait, Jesus. I want to go with You! You just healed me. You took away all my shame. You took away all my problems. You cast out all the demons. You loved me like nobody else has ever loved me. Please, I want to go with You!"

And Jesus said...

Wait for it...

"No. You can't come."

What? That's not the Jesus we read about, is it? I mean, this is the Jesus who normally says, "Come. Follow me. I'll make you a fisher of men." But Jesus said no. Why? Jesus said, "No, don't come with me. I want you to go to your village. I want you to go to your family, and I want you to tell them what God has done for you today."

Do you realize what Jesus did? He developed a disciple who was going to go and develop more disciples. That is what the Scripture says—the man, who was now healed completely, went back to his village and preached to a region of ten cities. Ten cities! Jesus picked up this guy whom nobody wanted, whom everybody rejected, and He healed him. He cast out the demons, and He loved him. Then Jesus sent him out to tell other people about how awesome God is.

This guy knew nothing, right? He didn't have a degree from a Bible college. He didn't have training from Jesus; he met Him one time. All he had was his own testimony and his own encounter with the Lord. He knew Jesus was amazing. He knew Jesus was God, and he had to go tell everybody else about Him. Jesus used him to transform ten different cities. In a snap of Jesus' fingers, the man went from being a lunatic to being a

Christian extremist. No education. Just spiritual power. And it all came from Jesus.

If God could use that man, He can use you. There's no doubt about it!

Our power springs from our relationship with Jesus. Nothing else. Each of us has the ability from the beginning to share what we have been given by a wondrous Savior!

You might be thinking, *what about the women? We have a lot of women in the church, and a lot of people say they aren't allowed to do much.*

To answer that question, I will tell you another story about Jesus because, really, it's all about Him.

One day Jesus was walking towards a village. Outside of the village was a well. It was in the middle of the day, and nobody hauled water from the well in the middle of the day because it was so hot. They either went in the morning or in the evening.

Jesus was there...along with one woman. Why was she there alone and in the middle of the day? Because nobody wanted to be around her. She was an outcast. She had been married to five men, and the man whom she was living with at that time wasn't her husband. In that day and in that culture (much like many cultures around the world today), this woman was rejected. People looked down on her and called her a sinner. They called her dirty and worthless.

Then Jesus spoke to her. He broke all social barriers. A Jew was not supposed to talk to a woman in public, let alone a sinful woman like this one, let alone a Samaritan woman. But Jesus did. Why? Because Jesus loves all of us. He wants all of us.

We're all His children. The God of the universe, the God who created the world, stepped down out of heaven and became a man. He talked to people whom no one else would talk to in that culture, and He continues to do that today. He loves people no one else will love. He serves people no one else will serve. He was the first Christian extremist.

After He talked to the woman, she went back to her village and told everybody about Jesus. John 4:39 says, "Many of the Samaritans from that town believed in him because of the woman's testimony…" She told her story about what God had done for her, and God used her to change an entire village.

No matter what your past is, no matter the sins with which you've been strug-gling, no matter your education level, God can use you.

If you are a woman and you are reading this, know that if God can use that woman—a sinful woman who was rejected and had a bad past—then He can use you. There's no doubt about it.

She had a horrible past. Five marriages. A sixth man sharing her bed. A bad reputation. It didn't matter. Jesus showed up, changed her heart in one conversation, and used her to trans-form an entire village!

No matter what your past is, no matter the sins with which you've been struggling, no matter your education level, God can use you. Think about this: all of Jesus' disciples were fishermen, tax collectors, and sinners. He called people from all walks of life. He called prostitutes to follow Him. He called sinners to follow Him—people nobody else wanted. Jesus healed them, cleansed them, and used them mightily.

If God can use people like that—if God can use people like me—then He can use you. Are you willing to step up, no matter what your past is like, no matter what your education level? If so, then say, "I am going to surrender my life to Jesus so He can use me to do big things just like He did with these people in the Bible. I will be a Christian extremist."

If God is with you, you need nothing else.

The truth is, we're all nothing without Christ anyway. The evangelist Reinhard Bonnke says, *"We're all zeroes."*

We're all zeroes, but Christ represents the number one. When we "zeroes" stand next to Christ, what does that make us? Tens—a one next to a zero is a ten. If another zero comes, we are 100. And if another comes, we are 1,000. Then 10,000, and then, 100,000—1,000,000—10,000,000—100,000,000—and so on. You get the idea!

Christ is number one! He gives all of us "zeroes" power and significance. Every zero is important. He gives each of us worth and value. With Christ, we become strong and powerful.

When many zeroes are together under His leading, we become unstoppable.

But remember, if we take away Christ, we all become nothing again: 00000000000. No matter how many zeroes are together, if there is no "1" leading them, they are worth nothing. If we keep Christ number one in our lives and follow after Him, we can do amazing things. He gives us worth and value. He gives us power! John 15:5 says, "Apart from me, you can do nothing."

Everything—Jesus = Nothing
Jesus + Nothing = Everything

We have it all with Him, and nothing without Him. He is truly all we need. Since our ministry does not depend on our own abilities and strength, but His, we can do whatever He has called us to do.

We can do this. Let's get started.

If a man hasn't found
something worth dying
for, he is not fit to live.

—MARTIN LUTHER KING, JR.

Chapter

The Spark of Extreme Commitment

ERNÁN CORTÉS WAS a Spanish conquistador in the 1500s. After some time as a colonist in Cuba, he set sail with the vision of claiming Mexico for Spain, and he conquered the Aztec Empire in the process. The Aztecs were known to be fierce and deadly; no one had ever even come close to defeating them. Their very name brought fear into the hearts of men and women in the area. They had subjugated tribe after tribe to their dominion.

According to legend, they built a city from pure gold. Diamonds, jewels, and many other amazing treasures could be found in the city as well. Cortés made a commitment to go and take it all for Spain. For him, the reward far outweighed the risk.

When they landed on the shores of Mexico, his men were tired and scared. He was worried that when they saw the savagery of the Aztec warriors, they would turn and run back to their boats and retreat. To ensure that this didn't happen, he commanded his leaders, "Go and burn the boats!"

"What? Burn the boats? That's our only way home!"

I said, "Burn the boats!"

Cortés did not want retreat to be an option. He did not want the comforts of the colonies or Spain to tempt him or his men to run away. He wanted his men to have two options only: conquer or die! He would not allow retreat. In response to Cortés' command, the leaders burned and sank their own ships, sparing none.

The third option—retreat—was now gone. If they wanted to stay alive, they had only one direction they could go: inland— with swords in their hands and victory on their hearts. This *extreme commitment* was the spark his men needed.

In the spirit of Cortés, it's time to burn our boats!

Hernán Cortés and his men conquered the Aztec Empire. They took the land and came back victorious. The Mexico that we know today is the result of this man, his army, and their focused commitment.

Think about this with me for a minute. What things in your life right now are tempting you to give up your commitment to live an extreme Christian life? What things continue to pull you away? In the spirit of Cortés, it's time to burn our boats! Get rid of them. Remove retreat as an option.

In Scripture, Jesus talks about two roads: the narrow one and the wide one. According to Francis Chan, we've created another road. A third road. The middle road, with no extreme on either side. An existence of just getting by. Jesus calls this "lukewarm Christianity" in Revelation.

You don't want that, do you? You don't want to be just so-so, do you? Then it's time to burn your boats! Shut down that third road. Destroy it. Burn the bridge that gets you there. Take that option away. You're either all-in or all-out. Make a decision. Make a commitment, and burn your boats. Stick to it!

In his writings, Robert Murray M'Cheyne, who was a minister in the Church of Scotland from 1835 to 1843, tells a story of a village in Africa that consisted entirely of lepers. It was surrounded by high walls and had only one door. If anyone in the surrounding areas had signs of leprosy, they were taken to this village, thrown inside, and never allowed to come back out. The door was locked from the outside.

Two young Moravian missionaries heard about this place and wanted to serve the lepers there. They arrived and asked if they could enter the village so they could serve the people. The locals responded, "You can go in. But once you do, you cannot ever come back out! That's a one-way door."

That day, the two young men decided that they were ready to burn their boats. They made a commitment to go in and share the love of Christ with the lepers, knowing that they could never return. That's extreme commitment. That's extreme love. And that's what Christian extremists do. They burn their boats. They forsake everything to follow Jesus to the ends of the earth. They live out Jesus' words when He tells us in Luke 9:62, "No one who puts a hand to the plow and looks back is fit for service in the Kingdom of God."

What's holding you back right now? What's keeping you from truly committing yourself to following Jesus? What is tempting you to retreat? Hand it over to Jesus. Burn your boats! And then follow Him wherever He calls you to go.

Have you ever heard the story behind the famous old hymn "I Have Decided"? According to tradition, the song was originally written in India. More than one hundred years ago, missionaries from Wales traveled to northeast India to preach the Gospel of Jesus Christ.

One missionary went to a tribal village in the state of Assam. He was rejected over and over again, but finally, by God's grace, he was able to lead one family to the feet of Jesus Christ. The tribal chief found out about the conversion and wanted to make an example of the family who had turned against their local gods. The chief dragged the family into the center of the village and told the husband that he had one last chance to recant his faith.

The chief gave word to the archers in the village that, if the man did not deny Jesus, they were to shoot his children. The man looked at his children with love in his eyes and explained to them why he could not deny Christ. Then he looked to the chief and boldly proclaimed, "I have decided to follow Jesus. No turning back, no turning back."

After he uttered those words, the archers shot both of his children, and they died before his eyes. The chief then gave the man another opportunity. He said, "All you have to do is deny Jesus! If you don't, we will kill your wife next."

The man looked at his wife and told her good-bye. Then he boldly proclaimed, "Though none go with me, still I will follow. No turning back. No turning back."

After he spoke those words, they killed his wife. As he looked down at the bodies of his wife and children, he knew it was his turn to give his life for Jesus. He shouted out at the top of his lungs, "The cross before me, the world behind me! No turning back! No turning back!"

Instantly, the archers shot the man and his body fell where the rest of his family members were already lying. As soon as the man hit the ground, the chief's heart began to change. He began to doubt his own faith. He began to think, *This Jesus must be real. Why would a man give his entire family and his own life for someone who wasn't real? I must know more about this Jesus!*

Because of one family's bold stand, a spark spread from the tribal chief to the entire tribe. The chief and many from the tribe members accepted Jesus—all because of one family's incredible sacrifice and amazing commitment.

You are a new creation. You are a hero of the faith

What is the secret of this commitment? Where does it truly come from? Identity. Our identity in Christ. If we don't know who we are, we won't know how to live. If the world is a stage, then we must know our role. This role and identity will lead us to extreme action.

So who are you, really? You are the light of the world. The salt of the earth. God's chosen one. Men are the princes of God's Kingdom, and women are His princesses. We are all heirs of the throne of God. You have been adopted as His child. You are truly a child of the King. You are saved, sanctified, and forgiven. You are a new creation. You are a hero of the faith.

When we look back on history, we talk about Calvin and Luther and Wesley and Spurgeon and many others. In two hundred years, if Christ waits that long to come back, believers will be talking about you, the things you did, and the extreme love you showed. They will be talking about how a few Christian extremists changed the world.

If we want this to be true, then we must stop living a so-so life. Stop balancing on the line between good and evil. Go all in! Jump into the deep end. Give it everything we've got. Open our lives fully to Jesus.

Let's burn our boats. Leave it all behind. "Throw off all the sin that entangles us, and run this race with all we have" (see Romans 12:1). Get filled, and burn with the Holy Spirit's power. May He ignite us with His love and grace, boldness, mercy, power, courage, and passion, so we can stand tall and be a spark for other people.

Remember: your life is a match. Ignite the world. You are a son or daughter of the One True King. You have been knighted by the King Himself. You are a Christian extremist. Now go and live like it.

A Letter to the Sons and Daughters of the King

To Those on the Front Lines,
To the Sons and Daughters of our King, my Brothers and Sisters,
To the Faithful Scattered Across the World:

This is war.
The enemy doesn't want you to think so.
But it is.
He would much rather you stay blind and ignorant, thinking that God only desires your comfort and

happiness, that His only purpose for you is to be happy and healthy and wealthy and comfortable.

We must remember who we are.

And we must remember where we are.

This is enemy territory. We were sent here with a mission. A mission that has yet to be fulfilled. A mission where eternity hangs in the balance. Where souls are fought for and won. Where hearts are healed and restored. Where love is our weapon and Jesus the answer.

We must not forget.

We are ambassadors of the King. His children. His sons and daughters. Princes and princesses of the Kingdom. Where we walk, the Kingdom of God should be represented. Love and grace and mercy and forgiveness should be in our wake. Broken hearts should be mended, and lost souls saved. The kingdom of darkness should flee in terror, and the hearts of people all over the world should be raised from the dead.

The power and authority of the King Himself has been bestowed on each of us. Not because of our heroics or our strength but because of the sacrifice of our great King.

We are His chosen people. The bearers of light. The carriers of love. The family of God.

Therefore, we must fight. With all that we have and with all that we are. Fight.

Fight for the love of God and for the salvation of souls. Fight for the healing of the nations. Fight for justice and peace. Fight for orphans and widows. Fight for the poor and the oppressed. Our kingdom should never allow such injustices. Fight for the unborn and the slave. Speak for those who have no voice. Stand for those who are unable to stand. Touch the untouchable and love the unloved.

For the sake of the King and for the sake of the world, we must fight.

Therefore, we will break off the chains of mediocrity. Loose the shackles of conformity. Rise out of the pool of comfort. And go in the name of our great King and Savior, Jesus Christ. With His Spirit in us, His Word to guide us, the Father's love to fill us, and our fellow brothers and sisters at our side, we must go and never look back. Fight and never quit. Serve and never expect a return.

A hurting world waits.

In the name of our great King and for the glory of His great Kingdom,

Your fellow soldier and fellow heir of that coming Kingdom.

Extreme Challenge

At the end of every chapter for the remainder of the book, you will find an "Extreme Challenge" section. In this section we are going to challenge you to begin to live out the teachings about which you are reading. The goal is to stretch you and to give you solid action steps to take in your life so that you can begin the journey of becoming a Christian Extremist! Let's get started!

A. Take a moment right now to list the things that are holding you back from truly following Christ with all you have. Take a minute, be silent before God, and ask Him to speak to you.

1. _____

2. _____

3. _____

4. _____

5. _____

Now, make a decision. Change whatever you need to change so that you can give all you have to Jesus. Don't walk down the third road any longer. Burn your boats and live for Christ with all you have!

Make a plan to determine how you will change, asking God for help.

_____

_____

_____

_____

_____

B.   It's easy to forget who we truly are in Christ. When we do, we lose our passion, our power, and our focus. Every morning remind yourself who you truly are in Christ. Listen to the words the Father spoke to Jesus:

> "This is my Son, whom I love; with Him I am well pleased."

Or for the ladies:

> "This is my daughter, whom I love; with her I am well pleased."

In Christ, this is all true! You don't need to earn His love and grace. He loves you just because you are His child. We don't obey the Father so that He will love us; we love the Father because He already does. He chose us. Remind yourself of that every morning, and see the difference it makes in your life!

*You either allow the obstacles
in your life to be the excuse for
your failure or make them the
reason behind your success.*

—JOHN PIPER

*Anxiety does not empty
tomorrow of its sorrows,
but only empties today
of its strength.*

—CHARLES SPURGEON

Chapter

Common Barriers

WHAT'S STOPPING YOU from truly living an extreme life? What is holding you back from fully embracing the Christian extremist lifestyle?

In the last chapter, we talked about burning our boats—getting rid of the things that hold us back. In this brief section, we want to talk about some of the most common barriers that keep us from living the life that Jesus calls us to live.

Three Boats to Burn

Fear

"What if?"

That question completely paralyzes a Christian extremist in training. *What if people get upset with me? What if my family disowns me? What if people think I'm weird or crazy? What if I lose my friends? What if my boyfriend doesn't want to be with me anymore? What if my wife gets upset?*

What if _____?

What if _____?

What if _____?

You fill in the blanks.

The what-if game is never ending. Our minds can come up with millions of what-ifs. Here's the problem: ninety-nine percent of the things we worry about never happen. We need to change our perspective. This is how we burn the fear boat to the ground and get the what-ifs out of our heads. One small change can make all the difference.

Well, first let me tell you a quick story from the Old Testament we should know. You have probably heard the story of Shadrach, Meshach, and Abednego. They were the three young men who stood up against the king of Babylon. The king had issued a decree that everyone in the entire kingdom must bow down and worship a golden statue he had built. (It was a statue of him, by the way; no pride there, right?) So basically, the king commanded the entire kingdom to worship him.

This was all well and good for the average Joe. But not for three young Jews living there. They were dedicated to God. Their Law told them that they were to worship God and God alone. So when the time came, they didn't bow down. They didn't worship the king. While thousands of people were on their knees, these three young men stayed standing. The king tried to change their minds. He warned them that if they did not bow, they would all be executed.

Shadrach, Meshach, and Abednego did not ask "What if?"—they declared, "Even if!"

This was their response: "O Nebuchadnezzar, we do not need to defend ourselves before you. If we are thrown into the blazing furnace, the God whom we serve is able to save us. He will rescue us from your power, Your Majesty. But even if He doesn't, we want to make it clear to you, Your Majesty, that we will never serve your gods or worship the gold statue you have set up" (Daniel 3:16b-18 NLT). They were saying, "Our God can save us. But even if He doesn't, we would rather burn than bow down to your gods."

You know the rest of the story. They were thrown into a furnace, and they survived. God saved them, but they were ready for the consequences, either way. No matter what, they were not going to deny the Lord their God. Right here in this story is the small change, mentioned earlier, that we must make if we are going to burn the what-if game: Shadrach, Meshach, and Abednego did not ask "What if?"—they declared, "Even if!"

That's the stand you and I need to take if we are going to be true Christian extremists. Even if people think we're weird. Even if we lose some friends. Even if people get upset with us. Even if we lose our jobs. Even if our girlfriends and boyfriends break up with us. Even if the worst happens, we will follow Christ!

Even if, even if, even if…One small change in perspective can make all the difference. Instead of asking "What if?" let's begin to declare, like these three young men, "Even if!" That's what Christian extremists do. They remain faithful no matter what. They make the "Even if!" declaration.

Together, let's burn the boat of fear. This doesn't mean we will never feel afraid. It means we are ready to face that fear with courage, no matter what comes our way. Courage can be summoned only in the face of fear. Boldness can emerge only when you feel afraid.

Take a stand. No matter what. Even if.

Idolatry

In the previous story, a physical idol was standing in front of the three boys. That's not always the case. You don't have to have an idol in front of you to commit idolatry. *True idolatry is placing anything above and before God.*

Is there anything you love more than Jesus? Is there anything you give more time and attention to than Him? Is there anyone whose words carry more weight than Jesus Himself in your life? Is there anything you would not give up if Jesus asked you to?

Idols. They are all around us. John Calvin used to say that the human heart is an idol factory. We can make idols out of anything: people, sports, money, jobs, food, possessions, homes. Anything. The idols in our hearts can hold us back from jumping all-in with Jesus, and we can't bargain with idols. They must be destroyed. They must be burned. I'm not implying that, if a person is an idol, we must destroy our relationship with him or her. What I am saying is this: almost every idol we have in our lives is a good thing that we've turned into a god of some kind. Children? Great blessing! Money? Great blessing! Work? Great blessing!

Who or what is on the throne of your heart? Who or what is your King?

But as Scripture says, the problem surfaces when we begin to worship the created things of this world rather than the Creator (Romans 1:20-23). Are we worshipping the gifts God has given us more than the great Giver Himself? It would take an entire book to lead you through the process of destroying idols in your life and putting them back into the proper places in your heart. Many others have done a much better job than I can. So in this section, I'll just say that the big question is this: who or what is on the throne of your heart? Who or what is your King?

Think and pray about that. I'm sure a person or a thing immediately came to your mind. For whom or what are you living? Who or what is truly in control of your life? If it's not Jesus, then you've got a big problem. Before you can ever step into an extreme Christian life, you need to get that person or thing off the throne and into its proper place. Only One is worthy to sit there. Only One is worthy of truly ruling your life—and that is Christ Himself. He paid for the privilege with His life.

Take some time right now to think through and pray about who or what is on the throne of your heart. This is far too important to just skip over. List your idols here:

1. _____.

2. _____.

3. _____.

4. _____.

5. _____.

Now, imagine yourself with Jesus at your side as you take each of these things off the throne in your heart, one by one, and place them in front of the throne. They are meant to worship or help you worship the King of Kings. They should be on their knees in front of the throne, not sitting on it.

Once you have worked your way in prayer through each idol give Jesus the scepter. Give Him the throne. Let Him be in charge. Picture Him as He sits down as the Ruler of your life. Spend some time worshipping Him. Spend some time apologizing for not giving Him His rightful place in your life. Hear Him tell you that His grace is sufficient for you, that His love covers these mistakes, and then worship Him some more for His great mercy. Do this every day because you can be sure of this: a rebellion will be stewing among those former idols. Every day, keep them in their proper place.

For more clarity and depth on this topic, we recommend *Counterfeit Gods* by Timothy Keller and *Gods at War* by Kyle Idleman.

Comfort

This is probably the hardest boat to burn. We Westerners love comfort. Sometimes what is holding us back is not fear and not idolatry. Sometimes it's just plain laziness and apathy. We just don't care about anyone but ourselves.

To burn this boat, we have to be willing to get uncomfortable. We have to be willing to step out of our comfort zones. We have to open our hearts to what is happening around us in the world. If you aren't willing, then nothing will really help, but if you are, keep reading.

I am going to try to open your eyes to what is going on around the world with the hope that it will rock your heart so much that you can no longer sit still. William Wilberforce, an

English politician and philanthropist who led the movement to abolish the slave trade, said, "You may choose to look the other way, but you can never say again that you did not know." This is my prayer—that after reading the following section, none of us will be able to just sit still. We can no longer say that we never knew. We can no longer plead ignorance. The only answer from this point on will be selfishness and apathy.

Let's begin the journey. It may feel a bit like Eustace in Narnia when Aslan rips the scales off his dragon-like back, but it will be worth it.

The Need to Make a Difference Is Urgent

It isn't difficult to find statistics about the extreme suffering people endure worldwide each day:

- According to Bread for the World, 2.6 million children die each year as a result of hunger-related causes. That's 7,123 a day, 300 an hour, and five every minute.[1]

- The World Health Organization reports that an estimated 250,000 to 500,000 vitamin A-deficient children become blind every year, and half of them die within twelve months of losing their sight.[2]

- One of the largest smuggling businesses in the world generates billions of dollars each year. It's not the Mafia, and it's not drugs. It's human trafficking, often for the purpose of sex slavery. The International Labour Organization reports that $99 billion per year comes from commercial sexual exploitation.[3] The average age of those being trafficked is twelve years old.[4] These girls and boys should be freshmen in high school, not servicing men for money. This isn't a choice. Most of these children have been kidnapped and used against their will. Some of them are forced to service, on average, twenty to forty-eight men per day.[5]

- Men are taking "sex tours" to distant countries to look for younger and younger children. It is estimated that up to fifteen thousand girls are trafficked each year from Nepal across the border into India where they are sold into Indian brothels and forced to become prostitutes. These girls are as young as seven-years-old although the average age has remained about fifteen.[6]

- Studies show Southeast Asian countries—particularly Cambodia, the Philippines, and Thailand—are the most common destinations for child sex tourism.[7]

- Since the 1990s Joseph Kony, founder of the guerilla organization known as the Lord's Resistance Army (L.R.A.), has killed and abducted around thirty thousand children who were forced, often under the threat of dismemberment or death, to join the LRA.[8]

- Approximately 1.5 million children in developing countries die each year of preventable diseases like pneumonia, diarrhea, measles, and polio. That means one child dies every twenty seconds from a disease that could have been prevented by a vaccine.[9]

- More than one-third of the world's population is unreached by the Gospel. They have never heard the name of Jesus.[10] Many of them do not even know a single Christian. And each day, 44,000 people die without hearing the Good News.[11]

He didn't die so that you would sit back and relax. He died so that you could finally live.

What do you feel when you read all of this? Anger? Sadness? Sickness? True Christian extremists don't just feel these things. They take action. Don't listen to that still, small voice of comfort. Jesus is calling you to something more. He is calling you to be extreme. He didn't die so that you would sit back and relax. He died so that you could finally live. There are enough people sitting on their tails, not doing anything. That's not the call of a Christian extremist.

Christian extremists allow their feelings to catapult them into action. Do something. Buy a plane ticket. Contact a missionary and schedule a trip to visit him or her. Travel the world and see these conditions for yourself.

Sometimes we ask, "Why does God allow these things? Why doesn't He do something?" I think He is asking us the same question. When we ask, "Where are You, God?" He responds by asking, "No. Where are *you*?"

May we no longer succumb to the temptation of comfort. May we stand up and begin to boldly address the problems in this world. May we burn the things that are holding us back and begin to sacrificially transform this world. That's what Christian extremists do—they put other people's needs above their own desires. How can other people be going without their daily needs when we are swimming in abundance?

The Christian extremist shouts, "No more! This will not be the case with me!" Or will you sit back and relax and let other people handle these worldwide iniquities? The choice is yours. As mentioned earlier, you can choose to turn your head and ignore these things, but you can never again say that you didn't know about them.

Extreme Challenge

If you haven't done so already, go back to the idol section of this chapter and take time before Jesus to dethrone each of the idols in your heart. This is by far the most important thing you can do right now. If you've already done it, then congratulations! You've already finished your extreme challenge for this chapter!

Many years ago, Dr. Kent Keith wrote the following poem entitled "The Paradoxical Commandments." It was so influential that Mother Teresa hung it on the wall of her room in Calcutta.

The Paradoxical Commandments

People are illogical, unreasonable, and self-centered.
Love them anyway.

If you do good, people will accuse you of selfish
    ulterior motives.
Do good anyway.

If you are successful, you will win false friends and
    true enemies.
Succeed anyway.

The good you do today will be forgotten tomorrow.
Do good anyway.

Honesty and frankness make you vulnerable.
Be honest and frank anyway.

The biggest men and women with the biggest ideas
    can be shot down by the smallest men and women
    with the smallest minds.

Think big anyway.

People favor underdogs but follow only top dogs.
Fight for a few underdogs anyway.

What you spend years building may be destroyed
overnight.
Build anyway.

People really need help but may attack you if you do
help them.
Help people anyway.

Give the world the best you have, and you'll get
kicked in the teeth.
Give the world the best you have anyway.

Radical obedience to Christ
is not easy... it's not comfort,
not health, not wealth, and
not prosperity in this world.
Radical obedience to Christ
risks losing all these things.
But in the end, such risk
finds its reward in Christ.

He is more than enough for
us. My biggest fear, even
now, is that I will hear
Jesus' words and walk away,
content to settle for less than
radical obedience to Him.

— DAVID PLATT

Chapter

The Spark of
Extreme Obedience

I'T'S EASY FOR us to talk about Jesus and read our Bibles and
Christian books like this one, but when it comes to actually
putting it all into practice, that's another ball game, isn't it?
We all desire to live an extreme life. But somewhere between
good intentions and incredible actions, we fall off the horse.
We find ourselves believing much but doing little.

I'm inclined at this point to tell you what the Greek word for
"obey" is and tell you what it means and why that is important,
but is that truly necessary? We have enough scholars in the

world. What we need is more obedience. Let's make it simple. The word obey means, "Just do it!" We all know that, right? Pretty simple. The truth is, we must simply do what God calls us to do.

> Being obedient requires that we surrender to His will and do what He wants us to do—not what we want to do.

When we simply do what God tells us to do, we glorify Him; we also reap the blessings He bestows on us as obedient children. Jesus tells us in John 14:23 that "Anyone who loves me will obey my teaching. My Father will love them, and we will come to them and make our home with them."

Being obedient requires that we surrender to His will and do what He wants us to do—not what we want to do. This is always a challenge. Our God-given gifts and talents can be used for our own glory or for the glory of God. We must make that choice, and that choice colors all the many decisions we make as our lives progress. Our true submission to Christ is the deciding factor in this choice. Young Douglas Henry did not hesitate to surrender when he heard God's call as a quiet whisper, a plea, to help people suffering from leprosy. Mr. Henry was my (Ajai's) father-in-law. He has since gone to be with the Lord, but his story still inspires me to this day.

He grew up in an incredibly poor family in central India. His parents were Christians, so in spite of their poverty, they raised Douglas with strong principles and integrity. Their house was right next to the train tracks.

I remember him telling me about the first time he saw a man take his own life. The man was a leper. He walked out next to the tracks, waited for a train to pass, and threw himself in front of the speeding locomotive. He had lost all hope. No one loved him. No one cared for him. He was an outcast who was forgotten and unwanted.

My co-author, Josh Howard, writes:

Forgotten

Forgotten.

Drifting away into the sea of lost eternity.
Searching for significance,
Where love is a mirage in the distance.
Beckoning cold hearts that long for the warmth
Of one hand, one touch, one kiss, for some amount
    of timeless bliss
That will never be.

Forgotten.
While plummeting into the depths of prideful minds,
Where no one has a problem leaving them behind,
Hurt, scarred, abused, while singing tunes of blues
That are erased from our memory.
All throughout the centuries, it remains the same.

Forgotten.

Screaming at the top of their lungs to be heard.
Aching for someone, anyone, somewhere
To guide them back to shore,
So that they can finally spread their wings and soar—
Higher and higher and higher
Than they ever have before.

After seeing India's forgotten souls jump in front of moving trains over and over and over again, young Douglas Henry heard the still, small whisper of the Lord:

"Douglas, who will help these people?"

It was like the call to Isaiah. Not specific. Just a question asked out loud, "Who will go for Me?"

And like Isaiah, Mr. Henry stepped up to the challenge and obeyed the call of the Lord.

"I will go! I will help these people. Send me!"

After graduating from high school, Mr. Henry studied at the best medical college in India and then had the opportunity to go to England to study further. He was trained to perform reconstructive surgeries. He could have chosen to stay in England, or go to America, or move to a large city in India and make millions of dollars. But he had submitted his heart to Jesus, and his heart was for the forgotten, the outcast lepers of India. His heart deeply desired to obey the voice of the Lord.

He moved back to Chhattisgarh, India, close to the area where he grew up, to serve the leper community. He worked with a leprosy mission and spent his life serving "the least of these"—people literally and completely rejected from society by virtue of their illness.

In Matthew 25:40, Jesus says, "Whatever you do for the least of these, you do for me." Dr. Henry put legs and flesh and love and sweat and tears into this Scripture. He didn't just memorize it; he lived it. That's what Christian extremists do. They obey Jesus, no matter where it may lead them.

Isn't it funny how we can memorize Scripture like that and never do what it says? Francis Chan used the following excellent illustration in a sermon to drive this point home. He says this:

> What if I went into my home and told my teenage daughter, "Honey, go clean your room! It's a mess"? And then an hour later, my daughter comes into the living room and says, "Dad! Listen to this! I memorized what you told me to do...listen. I can say it word for word: 'Honey, go clean your room. It's a mess.' Isn't that awesome?! I worked really hard to get each word right!"
>
> How would I feel about that? I'd probably say something like, "Honey, if your room is not clean in five minutes, you're going to be in big trouble!"
>
> Or what if she said, "Well, before I clean it, I thought I would call a group of friends over, and we could talk about what you meant when you said, 'Go clean your room.' I'd like to study it a while first and make sure I know what you are talking about."

Again, she'd be in big trouble.

I don't care if my daughter memorizes what I said or if she studies what I said or if she writes down what I said. I just want her to obey. I want her to do it!

Francis's point is this: Do you think that we spend so much time studying and memorizing the Bible, listening to sermons, attending church, conducting small-group studies, and reading books about the Bible that we have forgotten the simplicity of just obeying what Jesus has called us to do?

Can you recite Matthew 28:18–20? You probably can. Part of it reads, "Go make disciples of all nations."

That's what Jesus says.

Here's the question: are we actually doing that? Are we actually committing our lives to obeying Jesus' final words? Are we obeying His other commands? Like "Love God with all you have" and "Love other people in the same way you want to be loved" and "Go make disciples of all nations."

Those three commands alone sum up the entire Bible: love God, love people, and make disciples. It's pretty simple, really, when you think about it. Why have we made it so complicated? When are we going to start putting these things into practice in our daily lives?

Many of us are sitting around, waiting to hear God's specific call on our lives. But are we even obeying the clear call that He's already given us in Scripture? We love to think about our specific, special call from God, but how can we expect to hear that call if we aren't obeying what He's already told us to do? Let's start there—with the commands of the Bible. I truly believe that as we are faithful in these commands, God will guide us more specifically. If we are not faithful over the straightforward things, how can He direct us into something greater?

Like a car driving at night, we can only see a few feet in front of us on this journey throughout life. But God sees the entire journey. He sees the big picture. When we obey God in the small things, we have no idea where it might take us. All we see is the immediate outcome, but God knows the full outcome. Let's take a look at what can happen when we obey our God who sees the future, no matter what.

Ritesh was raised in an incredibly poor family in central India. His father did his best to provide for the family, but it seemed that no matter how hard he worked, nothing was ever enough. Things got so bad that Ritesh's father had to do the unthinkable. With tears in his eyes, he sat Ritesh down and told him the bad news. "Today, I am taking you to a large farm on the other side of our state. The owner has promised that he will make a trade with me: one bag of rice for your service on his farm."

"Will I get to come home, Father?"

"No, son. I'm sorry. If I don't do this, our family will starve. You want to save your brothers and sisters, don't you?"

That day, Ritesh's father walked him to the farm owner's house and traded him for a bag of rice.

Ritesh was treated even worse than a slave. He was beaten almost daily. He slept with the animals. Some days he was fed, and some days he wasn't. He was in a child's hell.

But then one day, a preacher visited the farm. He saw the boy and found out what was happening. He immediately felt a call from the Spirit of God on his heart, "Do something."

Have you ever felt that call? "Son, just do something! Don't ignore this situation. Get up and move. Talk to that man. Talk to that woman. Look into this situation. Don't walk away!"

The preacher could have ignored the Holy Spirit's prompting. He could have thought, *this isn't my problem*. But he was a Christian extremist. He had extreme compassion and extreme love, and he wanted to obey Jesus, no matter what. So he did.

What happens when a Christian extremist shows up and obeys the call of the Lord?

After some negotiating, the preacher made a deal with the farm owner. The preacher gave him a small sum of money, and the farmer gave him the boy. He had been redeemed. The preacher immediately took Ritesh back to his family. He called us at Central India Christian Mission (CICM) right away and asked if our children's ministry could support Ritesh's family, and we did. Through this process, Ritesh became a follower of Jesus. As he got older, he decided to go to Bible college.

Today, Ritesh is one of our most dynamic evangelists. He has already planted five churches, baptized thousands of people, and saved many more children out of slavery.

Ritesh—sold for a bag of rice, bought back, and saved by Christ. Today he takes his story of redemption everywhere he goes. Twice sold. Twice bought. Twice redeemed. Once by man and once by Christ.

> Don't be afraid. Answer the call today
> and obey what God is asking you to do.

That's the power of Christian extremism. That's what happens when we obey the call of Jesus. The preacher didn't know what Ritesh would become. He did not know what the end of the story would be, but he listened to the Holy Spirit who did know. All we have to do is obey the One with the big picture. We need to listen to His voice and act upon the opportunities He puts in our lives. He will do the rest.

Today, Jesus is calling us to live our lives in obedience, just like the pastor in this story. We don't know what the outcome will be, but we do know that it will be an incredible journey with God leading us. Don't let anything hold you back. Don't be afraid. Answer the call today and obey what God is asking you to do.

Go.

Love God.

Love people.

Make disciples.

Extreme Challenge

We are going to break this challenge into two parts:

A. **Loving God**—As we've already discussed, your relationship with Jesus is the most important thing in your life.
How are you doing with that? In order to get a jump start
in strengthening your relationship with Him, here is your
challenge: in the next week, take one full day away from
everything. Go somewhere to be alone with Jesus. Take
your Bible. Take a journal and a pen, and that's all. Spend
time alone with Him. Ask Him to speak to you. Spend
time talking to Him about your life and about your heart.
If you are able, fast for the entire day. Take a few bottles
of water to stay hydrated, but leave food at home. Don't
allow this to be a one-time thing. Try to get away one day
every month to continue to strengthen your relationship
with Jesus. It's the most important thing that you can do.

B. **Doing What He Says**—During your time alone with
Jesus, take a moment and pray about the areas where you
are not obeying what God has called you to do. Obedience
really comes in two parts:

1. *Not* doing the things that God has told you *not*
to do. There are *Do Not's* in the Bible. You know,
sexual immorality, drunkenness, gossip. Are there
any areas of your life where you are living in disobedience? What are you currently involved in that you

shouldn't be? Take time now to confess these things before God and make a commitment that, with His help and power, you will get rid of these things in your life.

2. *Doing* the things that God *has* called you to do. These are the *Do's* in the Bible. Love your neighbor. Make disciples. Give to the poor. Things like that. The good things that God calls us to do. Are there any areas in your life right now where you are *not* doing the things that God has called you to do? According to Scripture, this is disobedience as well. James 4:17 says, "If anyone, then, knows the good they ought to do and doesn't do it, it is sin for them." Disobedience is disobedience either way. Are you doing things that you shouldn't? You are disobeying. Are you *not* doing things that you should do? You are disobeying. Take time right now to sit quietly before God and ask Him to reveal to you the things that you should be doing, but currently are not. Make a commitment now to start living out these things.

You can make a list of them here:

_____

_____

_____

Four Voices We Must Hear

This example has been used by Brother Ying Kai, who is a missionary in China, to inspire people to obey Jesus and share His love with everyone. God has used Brother Ying to ignite a movement in China that has baptized over one million people. I hope this inspires you in the same way it has me. The following is my version of Ying Kai's Four Voices.

Ying Kai's Four Voices

Over and over again, Scripture has called us to share the love of Jesus with those around us.

Today, there are four voices that I want you to hear that are calling out to you.

Four voices that are telling you to go.

Four voices that are urging you to share the love of Jesus with those around you.

1. A Voice from Heaven

In Isaiah 6, Isaiah has a vision of God seated on His throne in heaven. God is calling out in a loud voice, "Whom shall I send and who will go for us?"

In other words, God is calling out to us and saying, "Who will go tell people about me? Who will be my witnesses? Who will go make disciples? Who will tell people about my son Jesus? Who will go and tell the world?"

Isaiah stood up and immediately proclaimed, "Here am I! Send me!"

Today, I want you to hear the same voice that Isaiah heard. Today, God is calling out asking the same question, "Whom shall I send, and who will go for us? Who will go and tell people about my love?"

May you have the same answer that Isaiah had.

"I am here, Lord! Send me! I'll go for you! I'll tell people about you! I will tell people about your love! I will go to the nations for you!"

2. A Voice from Hell

There is a voice from above, but there is also a voice from below. In Luke 16, Jesus tells a story about a rich man and a poor man. The poor man is a faithful follower of God, but the rich man is not. One day, they both die. The poor man goes to heaven, but the rich man goes to hell.

The rich man cries out from hell, "Please send someone to warn my friends and my family so that they will not come to this place!"

Today, there are many people in hell who have died without Jesus, and they are crying out to you. "Please go tell my friends! Tell my family. Warn them about this place. Tell them that Jesus is the true God. Tell them that they must put their faith in Jesus so that they won't come to this awful place. Please! Go tell them!"

Listen to their voices today.

3. A Voice from Outside

In Acts 16, Paul has a vision of a man from a distant country. In the vision, the man is crying out to Paul saying, "Please come and help us. Come and preach to us. Come and save us!"

Right now, there are people in this world who are still alive, but they have never heard about Jesus. Can you hear their voices? Their souls are crying out to you just like they cried out to Paul, "Please come and save us. Tell us about Jesus. Come and help us!"

We must answer their call.

4. A Voice from Inside

The final voice that I want you to hear is a voice that has been calling you while you've been reading this. It is the voice of the Spirit inside of you. In 1 Corinthians 9:16, Paul says this, "...I am compelled to preach. Woe to me if I do not preach the gospel!"

He said that he was compelled. He just had to preach. The Spirit inside of him would not allow him to stay quiet. Jeremiah said that the Word of God was like a fire shut up in his bones. He just had to let it out!

There is a voice from heaven, a voice from hell, a voice from outside, and a voice from inside. All of them are calling you to go and preach the gospel. All of them are calling you to share the love of Jesus with your friends and family.

Can you hear their voices today? We must answer their cries. When we do, it will change our lives forever and the lives of those around us.

Not all of us can do great things. But we can do small things with great love.

—Mother Teresa

God's definition of what matters is pretty straightforward. He measures our lives by how we love.

—Francis Chan

Chapter

6

The Spark of Extreme Love

MANY YEARS AGO, a young Hindu woman was teaching in a Christian day school. Her husband and his family were incredibly strong in their Hindu faith, but they were fine with her teaching at the school as long as she didn't learn too much about Jesus.

After several months of working alongside Christians, the woman began to fall in love with Jesus. Without telling her family, she made a decision to follow Christ and to become a Christian. A few weeks later, her family found out about her decision, and they were outraged. They told her to leave the house immediately and said she was no longer welcome. They even threatened to kill her. She grabbed her infant son and ran out of the house. Because the family was so angry, she didn't even have time to put on her shoes.

After running for what seemed like hours and with many cuts and bruises on her feet, this young woman found her way to a Christian orphanage and gave her son to an American missionary whom, she hoped, would keep her son safe. The cuts on her feet became horribly infected, and the infection found its way into her bloodstream. A few weeks later, the young woman died.

The American missionary raised the little boy according to Christian principles. The boy grew up knowing the Lord Jesus and loving Him deeply. Upon his high school graduation, this little boy who had been saved by the American missionary became a teacher like his mother and began sharing the love of Jesus with other children.

That little baby boy's name was Samuel. And Samuel was my (Ajai's) grandfather.

Because one American missionary heard the call of God, left her home, and traveled to an impoverished village in India to take care of orphaned children, I can now say that I am a Christian leader. That's what Christian extremists do. They love with all they have and with all they are.

My grandfather was raised by a Christian extremist, and that changed everything.

Love.

Love is what drove the American missionary to India to save children's lives. That same love raised my grandfather. That love was then passed from my grandfather, to my father, and on to me. The love of Christ compels people to do extraordinary things, doesn't it?

In 2007, I (Josh) was traveling on a whirlwind tour to nine different countries. I was seeking the heart of God and trying to discern His call for my life. I knew I wanted to serve overseas; I just had no idea where. Kenya was one of the stops on this journey.

The people I was visiting took me to a slum in Nairobi called Mathare. I had never seen anything like it. Every time it rained, sewage flooded the streets and flowed into people's homes. Young children were digging through trash to find food. Ten people would live in a home that was the size of my bathroom in the United States. I was disgusted—not because of what I was seeing but because of the person I had been. Self-consumed. Prideful. Stingy.

People were living in such dire and needy conditions on the other side of the world, and I was complaining about not getting a new MacBook.

As I entered one home, a little girl greeted me with her arms raised high. She wanted me to pick her up. She wanted me to play with her, hold her, and jump up and down. I immediately held her in my arms. I mean, how can you resist such a cute little girl? The moment I started holding her, I noticed that my shirt was sopping wet. Her mother was mentally handicapped and unable to take proper care of her daughter. One of the ramifications of this was that the girl's diaper had not been changed in who knows how long. Urine was seeping out of her diaper and onto my shirt. The smell was overwhelming.

In my normal state, I would have been completely repelled. I would have looked like a father on a Hollywood movie trying to change a dirty diaper. You know, with the child held out at arm's length and a disgusted look on the man's face.

I don't know why, but in this situation I just couldn't let her go. For some reason, none of this bothered me. All I could do was hold the little girl tighter, and, believe me, it wasn't because of my wonderful, loving character. That wasn't true at all. The Spirit of God took over. His love began to control me. The Spirit of Christian extremism was upon me. After holding her for a while, it was time to leave and go to the next house. So I put her down, and as I walked away, the Spirit of God whispered in my ear in a way that only He can do, "I just showed you what My love looks like."

Wait...what?

> We are dirty and sinful and wretched, but when we run to the Father, He picks us up and loves us anyway. We don't make Him dirty. He makes us clean.

"You are just like that little girl, Josh. That's how great My love is. You run to me with your arms up and with things much dirtier than urine all over you. And you know what? I pick you up anyway. It doesn't bother Me at all. And instead of you making Me dirty, I make you clean."

I broke down. Tears began to flow. It was true. That little girl represented me. She represents all of us. We are dirty and sinful and wretched, but when we run to the Father, He picks us up and loves us anyway. We don't make Him dirty. He makes us clean.

That's how awesome His love is, and that's what extreme love looks like. Since we have been given such love, we are called to offer that same love back to those around us.

Here's a challenge: go get dirty. Play with kids in the slum. Love the sick and hurting. Visit the children's hospital. Let the love of God rub off on some other people. Remember, they don't make you dirty; His love through you makes them clean.

I once read a story about a fire that broke out in England many years ago. A two-year-old girl was trapped on the top floor of an apartment building. A man rushed in to save her and was able to bring her down to safety. He risked everything for the sake of this little girl's life.

Unfortunately, the little girl's family did not survive. She was placed in the custody of local authorities and put up for adoption. After a few weeks, several people applied to adopt the little girl. The news of her story had spread through newspapers everywhere; so many people's hearts were open to this poor girl's situation.

The local judge decided to have a hearing to decide who would be best to take care of the little girl. He personally decided to go through each application, interview the person, and make a decision about where the little girl would spend her life. Each applicant had an opportunity to prove to the judge why he or she would be a good parent to the little girl.

First up was a doctor. "I have plenty of money to take care of the girl. She will never go without if she stays with me!"

Next was a professor. "I am highly educated and have many degrees. I can ensure that the girl will get a wonderful education!"

Then there was a farmer. "I have hundreds of acres of land with plenty of food. The girl will never go hungry, and she will learn great discipline on the farm."

Last, a humble, poor man stepped forward. He said, "I may not have much money. I may not be educated or own land, but the proof of my love for this girl lies in the burns on my hands."

This was the man who had saved the girl from the burning apartment building. His love and sacrifice for her proved to the judge and to everyone in the courtroom where the girl should be placed.

> Christian extremists have burns on their hands. They have nails driven deep, just like their Savior.

We can say all day long that we love the poor. We can say we love the persecuted. We can say we love all of those around us. But here's a question that may be difficult to answer: *Where are the burns on your hands?*

Have you truly sacrificed for those you claim to love? Have you honestly placed them above yourself? Love is not just a feeling. Love is not just an emotion. Love is shown best by action.

Christian extremists have burns on their hands. They have nails driven deep, just like their Savior. Love is best seen in the context of hate. Hope is best seen in the context of darkness. Grace is best seen in the context of revenge.

Take Pastor Farhan, for example. A village in the state of Uttar Pradesh was known for criminal behavior. Almost every man who lived there was a wanted felon. Because Pastor Farhan was a Christian extremist, this is where he wanted to go and preach. He began to teach these men about Jesus every day. They were very close-minded at first, but slowly they began to open their hearts.

One day, Farhan went to preach in the next village which was just a few miles away. Two men in that village got incredibly angry that Farhan was teaching about Jesus, so they chased him out of the village with swords and guns in their hands. He ran back to the criminals' village, thinking he would be safe there, but the two men continued to pursue him. As soon as they entered the village, the local criminals saw that their new "guru" was being chased by angry men, so they grabbed them, took their swords and guns away, and tied them up.

Then the criminals did the unthinkable: they began to pray. But not to Jesus. They prayed to their Hindu gods and goddesses. This was their prayer: "Thank you for saving our new guru and for allowing us to capture the men who meant him harm. Since you saved him, we will now offer these two men to you as a sacrifice."

They were going to offer two human sacrifices to their local gods! Pastor Farhan immediately stood up and objected. "Men! We can't do that. Remember, I've been teaching you about Jesus, and Jesus teaches us that we must love our enemies. We need to let them go."

The villagers couldn't believe it. "How can you let them go? They were going to kill you! We must teach them a lesson!"

Farhan stayed strong, "No. We must obey Jesus, and Jesus says to love our enemies. Let them go."

Farhan's stand in the name of Christ's love was the spark this village needed. The men let the two go, and that very day, because of Farhan's strong stand, the *entire* "criminal" village came to the feet of Christ. They shut down their local temple and became Christ-followers.

A movement started in this one village and has now reached more than one hundred other villages in the surrounding areas with the Gospel! One spark of extreme love changed an entire village and led to the salvation of hundreds of other villages. What can your spark of love do for the Kingdom?

Extreme Challenge

Do you realize that there are hundreds of people in your town who do not feel love on a regular basis? Elderly men and women in nursing homes often have no one to visit them. Children in orphanages have no one to hold them. Men and women are left on the streets with no home and no friends. It's time to put extreme love into action. Along with a few friends make a plan that in the next week you will visit one of these places in your area. Here are a few ideas to get you started:

A. Go to a local nursing home and ask the staff which residents do not have regular visitors. Spend time with these people for an entire afternoon. Play games with them, talk to them, and listen to music. Just love on them. Make a plan to go back on a monthly basis for a visit.

B. Volunteer at a local homeless shelter and love on the men and women who are in a rough season of life.

C.   Search on the internet to see where the nearest orphanage is located. Call them and set up a time when you could come and play with the children.

Or come up with your own ideas.

The main thing is this: go somewhere and love on some people who do not feel loved on a regular basis. Don't just do this one time and check it off of your bucket list. Make this a regular part of your walk with Jesus. Go and show people the love of Christ and watch as His love transforms the hearts of those around you.

*To be a Christian means
to forgive the inexcusable
because God has forgiven
the inexcusable in you.*

—C. S. LEWIS

Chapter

7

The Spark of
Extreme Forgiveness

MMANUEL AND HIS wife moved to a completely unreached area in India to start a new church. For the first several months, things went incredibly well. People came to Jesus, the Gospel was spreading, and they were able to launch a brand-new church.

One Sunday during worship, a group of men burst through the back door of the church with guns and swords. They wanted to stop these Christians from spreading their Western religion in their area. They grabbed Emmanuel and his wife, dragged them outside, and tied their feet with rope. Then they attached the other end of the rope to the back of a jeep and drove away. They dragged the couple behind the jeep through the jungle. The men thought it would kill the couple, but it didn't. They stopped the vehicle in a field and untied the ropes. Emmanuel and his wife were badly bruised and bleeding.

That wasn't enough for the extremists. They shouted at Emmanuel, "Deny Jesus *now*! If you don't, we will kill you and your wife!"

Emmanuel didn't speak. He knew in his heart that he would never deny Jesus, no matter what happened. They threatened him over and over again, but Emmanuel didn't budge. Because of his internal strength, they wanted to break him. They tied him to a tree and showed him a piece of paper. "If you don't deny Jesus, sign this paper, and become a member of our group, we will rape and kill your wife in front of your eyes! We know you're not afraid of death, but we know you love your wife. It's your choice, pastor. Deny Jesus, or watch us as we rape your wife."

Emmanuel was helpless. His hands were tied behind his back, and his entire torso was tied to a tree. He could do nothing.

If you are a man, what would you do in a situation like that? To protect your wife all you have to do is sign a paper. That's it. Sign and declare that you don't love Jesus anymore. If you are a woman, what would you do? Would you beg your husband to sign the paper?

Let me tell you what this woman did. She screamed at Emmanuel at the top of her lungs, "*Emmanuel!* Never sign that paper! Never deny Jesus! Let them do whatever they want to me. Just never deny our Lord!"

How many people do you know who could make a declaration like that?

Emmanuel didn't sign the paper that day. He watched with anger, rage, tears, and pain as four men started raping his wife. By the grace of God, the local villagers heard the screaming and ran to see what was happening. Because the four extremists were outnumbered, they ran away.

What would you do after that? Quit the ministry? Give up on God? Move to another location? I don't know what I would do, either. All I can tell you is what Emmanuel and his wife did. Two weeks later, they were back in the same church preaching the Gospel again! Two weeks! Can you believe that? What kind of determination is that? What kind of passion and love is that? Something that I'm not made of, certainly, but the story didn't end there.

Over the following weeks and months, the church's growth exploded. Tons of people started coming to Christ. The church continued to flourish. Not only that, but Emmanuel and his wife forgave the men who committed this horrible act. They invited them to parties. They said hello to them on the street.

Me? I would have wanted to kill those men. Emmanuel? He lived out Jesus' teachings about loving our enemies. He chose sacrifice and love over protection and revenge. As if that's not powerful enough, here's the best part of the story.

About a year after this event, Emmanuel held a New Year's Day worship service at his church—the same church where the attack had taken place. He invited the four men who had committed that horrible sin against him and his wife. *And they showed up.*

Not only did they show up, but they made a decision that day to follow Jesus, and they were baptized the same day.

This is what extreme love and sacrifice can accomplish for the Kingdom of God. This is what the grace of God truly looks like. This is what Christian extremists do: they forgive those whom others would deem unforgivable.

If God can save four men like that, He can save anyone you are trying to reach. Don't limit the reach of God's loving arms. Don't limit the extent of His amazing grace.

Here's what we know. If Emmanuel could overcome this horrible situation to build a thriving church, then what is stopping us? What is holding us back? When we put it into the proper context, our fear of rejection and difficulty pale in comparison to these leaders who have given it all for the Kingdom. When we place our situations next to theirs, nothing should seem impossible.

Where does forgiveness like that come from? How can someone love and forgive another human being who has brought so much pain and hurt to his family?

Jesus tells a story about a servant who owed a lot of money to his master. His master called him into his chambers and demanded that he pay back the money. The servant dropped to his knees and begged the master for mercy. The master was moved with pity for the man, so he forgave *all* of the debt the man owed. Imagine if your credit card company did that for you.

The servant was ecstatic. I'm sure he left feeling that a burden was lifted off his shoulders. He felt like he had a new chance at life. It was time to start over and make better decisions.

On the way home, the forgiven servant saw a man who owed *him* money. He stopped the man and told him that the loan had to be repaid. If the debt was not paid, the forgiven servant was going to call the authorities and have him placed in prison. The man, who was in the same situation that the forgiven servant had been in just moments before, dropped to his knees and begged to be forgiven for the debt. The forgiven servant refused and called the authorities.

Maybe the problem is that we still don't understand how much we have been loved and forgiven.

After some time, word got back to the master about what had happened. He was furious. Immediately, the master called in the servant whom he had forgiven. He said, "How wicked can one man be? You owed me more money than you could have ever repaid, and I cancelled all of the debt. And you couldn't forgive another man's much smaller debt? Because you treated him like this, I will treat you the same way. You will be put in debtor's prison until you can pay back every penny you owe me!"

The principle of the story is this: we need to learn to forgive in the way that we have been forgiven.

Maybe the problem with us is not that we don't love people enough. Maybe the problem isn't that we desire revenge. Maybe the problem is that we still don't understand how much we have been loved and forgiven. Sometimes we need to be reminded.

The greatest reminder we have ever received in India was through Mrs. Gladys Staines. Gladys and her husband, Graham, moved from Australia to India as missionaries several years ago. They were serving in the state of Orissa. They were serving the lepers of India who are considered untouchables. They were truly loving the unlovable and touching the ones who are untouchable in the eyes of the world.

Local extremists did not like their presence whatsoever. Number one, they were white, which to them meant the spread of Western culture and the destruction of Indian culture. And number two, they were teaching people about Jesus which to the Hindu extremist is a Western religion.

One day, as Graham and his two sons were sleeping inside their jeep in a local village, extremists surrounded them. They locked them inside their jeep and set it on fire. Graham and his two sons were burned alive. The news spread throughout India. National news stations covered the funeral. They all wanted to hear Mrs. Staines's reaction. They wanted to hear what she had to say. They asked her to look into the camera and speak to the men who brutally killed her husband and two sons.

On camera, with millions of people watching, she declared, "I want these men to know that I forgive them." The reporters asked, "How can you forgive people who did such a horrible thing to your husband and two sons?" She responded, "It's because of the love of Jesus. He has forgiven us for all the horrible things we have done, and He teaches us to do the same. His love and forgiveness give me the strength to forgive those who have hurt us."

> They did not fight extreme hate with revenge. They fought extreme hate with extreme love and forgiveness.

And then, to the shock of the crowd, she held her only daughter's hand, and together they began to sing the classic gospel song "Because He Lives" by the Bill Gaither Trio

This live testimony of a mourning wife and mother shook the soul of India. It was plastered all over the front pages of newspapers all over the country and on every news channel. You could not turn on the television without seeing this woman's amazing forgiveness.

She and her daughter were true Christian extremists. They did not fight extreme hate with revenge. They fought extreme hate with extreme love and forgiveness. They were truly disciples of our Lord Jesus who on the cross looked up to heaven, after being beaten, spit upon, and tortured horribly, and shouted, "Father, forgive them, for they do not know what they are doing" (Luke 23:34).

You see, when we open our hearts to the Father's forgiveness and let it wash all of our sins away, we then have the Spirit's power to offer that same forgiveness back to those who harm us. Revenge destroys. Forgiveness heals.

Choose which side you want to be on.

Extreme Challenge

A. Take a minute to truly think about the forgiveness Jesus has given you. He has taken all of your shame and sin away. He has washed it all clean. He loves you with a love that can never be taken away. Nothing you do can make Him stop loving you. Nothing you do is too horrible for His grace and forgiveness.

B. Meditate on that. Thank Him for that. Close your eyes and picture His love and forgiveness filling you up from the top of your head to the tips of your toes. Imagine that you are diving into a pool that is full of God's love and grace. Let it wash over you. Let it cover you. Let it fill you up.

C. Now that you have really felt and experienced God's love, it is time to give it back to those who have hurt you.

Make a list of people who have hurt you, and you've never forgiven them:

1. _____

2. _____

3. _____

4. _____

5. _____

It won't be easy, but that's what Christian extremists do. They give their hurt and their pain over to God and trust that He will take care of it. Leave justice in God's hands. Take time to pray for each person. Ask for Jesus' help to forgive them. If you are able, call them and tell them that you have forgiven them. If not, write them an e-mail or a letter. If they are no longer alive, just say it out loud as if you are speaking to that person: "Because of God's love in my life and the forgiveness I have received from Him, I forgive you in the same way I have been forgiven."

Let this be a new day and a new beginning. You are now filled with love, grace, and forgiveness. It is not by your power that forgiveness can be given but by the love and grace of your King.

What Does Forgiveness Really Mean?

What does it truly mean when you say you forgive someone? It doesn't mean that what they did was acceptable. It doesn't mean that you will be one hundred percent okay from that point on, either, but it does mean that you will abide by these four promises of forgiveness:

1. I will no longer dwell on this incident and picture revenge.

2. I will not bring this incident up again to use it against you.

3. I will no longer talk badly about you to other people.

4. I will no longer allow this incident to stand between us.

When you truly forgive someone as God forgave you, it also means you let go of the desire to even the score—regardless of how egregious their crime against you was. God does not measure the severity of our sin before He forgives us. We need to forgive others in the same manner.

Elijah was a man just like us. He prayed earnestly that it would not rain, and it did not rain on the land for three and a half years.

—JAMES 5:17

Chapter

The Spark of Extreme Prayer

AVE YOU EVER taken a minute to stop and think about this verse? It should change our entire prayer lives. Elijah was a man just like us. Hannah was a woman just like us. They prayed, and something miraculous happened.

See if the following events don't inspire your prayer life:

- Moses prayed, and water bubbled up from a rock in the ground.

- Joshua prayed, and the sun stood still.

- Hannah prayed, and God gave her Samuel, who led Israel closer to God.

- David prayed, and Goliath was defeated.

- Elijah prayed, and fire fell from heaven.

- Daniel prayed, and God locked the mouths of lions.

- Peter prayed, and blind eyes were opened.

- Paul prayed, and chains were broken.

- Jesus prayed, and a dead man named Lazarus walked out of his grave.

- Jesus prayed, and lepers became clean.

- Jesus prayed, and thousands of people were fed from a little boy's sack lunch.

- Jesus prayed, and a funeral procession was turned into a victory parade.

- Jesus never taught his disciples how to preach, but He did teach them how to pray.

None of these things happened because of the power of individual men—with the exception of Jesus. He was God-in-flesh. These things happened because of the power of God. It's not how great the men were or how great their prayers were—it is about to whom they were praying.

Have you stopped to consider who you are praying to every day? The God who did all of these things is the same God you are speaking to every time you pray. Shouldn't that make you consider more carefully how you are praying?

Being a Christian extremist changes the way you pray.

At times, our prayers sound like this: "God, could you kinda, maybe, if You can and if it's Your will, pretty please with a cherry on top, maybe heal my friend? I don't want to bother You or anything. And if not, at least be with the doctors and help them do a good job. Amen."

What kind of prayer is that? Let's pray bold prayers! That's what Christian extremists do. They pray boldly. They pray to the God who created the heavens and the earth. They pray to their Father who always listens. They pray to the King of Kings and the Lord of Lords, who has all power and authority.

Being a Christian extremist changes the way you pray. We've experienced this firsthand time and time again. Let me tell you a few stories to light the fire a bit.

More than thirty years ago, my wife, Indu, and I (Ajai) were living in a large city in central India. A local chief inspector was connected to an extremist group and harassed us on a daily basis because of our faith. He demanded that we give him thousands of dollars or else he would do horrible things to our family. We did not want to give in to his demands, but we were scared of what he might do. So we did what every other Christian extremist would do—we prayed! If God can shut the mouths of lions, he can shut the mouth of the police inspector, right?

At first, things didn't get any better. As a matter of fact, they got worse. One day, he called me and gave one last threat: "If you don't pay the money, I know where your daughter goes to school. It would be a pity if something happened to her on the way home, wouldn't it?"

You think this stuff happens only in the movies? Think again.

The amount of money he demanded was more than we had, and there was no way we could get it. We feared for our daughter's life.

The man set a deadline. "By twelve noon on Thursday, if you don't have the money, something bad is going to happen to your daughter."

So we prayed more. We prayed harder. We prayed boldly. Noon came and went. We heard nothing from the police inspector. A few days later, after not hearing from him, I finally discovered what happened. The inspector had gone to his office that Thursday morning and sat at his desk. Around noon, he began to have massive chest pains, and he fell to the floor and died!

He was only in his twenties. No doctor could explain what had happened.

Did we pray for that to happen? Absolutely not. But God decided that the inspector's time of causing issues for Christians was over. We had prayed that God would take care of the situation—and He did. He is truly our protection and our shield.

Or take Mahipal, for example. Mahipal was a Hindu extremist who lived in New Delhi, India. He hated Christians.

Perhaps "hate" is a strong word, but it is not strong enough in this case.

He *despised* Christians.

He wanted to beat and kill every Christian he came across. As a matter of fact, he did. He beat, tortured, and killed countless believers. He even led an entire extremist group to do the same.

Eventually, Mahipal's wife became terribly ill. No doctor could help her. He prayed to all of the different gods and goddesses of the Hindu faith, but they were silent. He tried black magic. He went to witch doctors. He made sacrifices. Nothing worked.

One day, Mahipal was in his office, feeling down and depressed. He had nowhere to turn. Suddenly, a man walked in who was wearing all white clothes and a white turban on his head. The man sat down, and said, "Why do you look so sad? What's wrong?"

"My wife is dying, and I don't know what to do! Do you think I should be jumping up and down? What's wrong with you?"

The man replied, "Mahipal, God is alive. His name is Jesus. He can heal your wife."

Mahipal warned him, "Don't you know who I am? I lead a local extremist group. You'd better be careful mentioning the name of Jesus around here!"

The man said it again. "I'm just telling you, Jesus is your only hope. He can heal your wife. Pray to Him."

"Get away from here right now before I kill you! You know what I do to Christians, right?"

The man walked out of the office, and Mahipal never saw him again.

Mahipal went home, but he couldn't forget the man he had met that day. Mahipal had devoted his life to destroying people who talked about Jesus. But there he was, on his knees late at night, praying to the One whom he had fought against, "Jesus, if You're real and alive, like the man today said, please heal my wife. If You do, I will serve You forever."

I don't know how you feel about the theology of making deals with God in prayer, but, in this case, God answered Mahipal's prayer. The next morning, Mahipal woke up, and his wife was feeling better! Every day, she recovered more and more until she was finally completely healed. Mahipal kept his word. That Sunday, he tried to go to church. The pastor of the church he went to recognized him, cancelled the service, and ran away.

> That's what the spark of extreme prayer can do! It can melt the hardest of hearts and open doors that no one thinks possible.

So Mahipal tried a different church the following week, and the same thing happened. Finally, he was able to talk to a pastor who told him about Central India Christian Mission. He came to our main campus, received training, and became a pastor.

This was truly the Apostle Paul's story all over again. From Hindu extremist to Christian extremist. That's what the spark of extreme prayer can do! It can melt the hardest of hearts and open doors that no one thinks possible.

Why not start praying bold prayers and see what God does? In the words of Oscar Muriu in Nairobi, Kenya, "Pray prayers that make God sweat!"

That's what Christian extremists do; they pray as if it all depends on God, and they work as if it all depends on them.

Extreme Challenge

A. You've heard of BHAGs, right? Big, hairy, audacious goals. Well, Christian extremists live by BHAPs—big, hairy, audacious prayers.

Take a moment right now to list five extreme prayers you are going to start praying on a daily basis. Make them so incredible and so huge that if they get answered, the only explanation will be that your incredible God miraculously answered you.

1. _____

2. _____

3. _____

4. _____

5. _____

Remember, Elijah and Hannah were humans, just like us. Go pray BHAPs and see what God does. Then go tell everyone!

B. What if, every morning, you prayed the prayer that Jesus told us to pray? "The harvest is plentiful, but the workers are few. Ask the Lord of the harvest, therefore, to send out workers into His harvest field" (Luke 10:2).

Pray for new workers. Pray that God would send new people to new locations to spread the Gospel.

Let's all commit to something. Based on Luke 10:2, let's set an alarm on our phones to remind us to pray every morning at 10:02 a.m. for more workers. Let's pray big prayers and see what the God of the Harvest will do!

A bold slave is more powerful than a timid king.

When you're bold, some people will think you're crazy, but it's more insane to be timid.

—Constance Chuks Friday

Chapter

The Spark of Extreme Boldness

SCREAMS. GUNS. MACHETES. Swords. Evil. Hatred.

It was all swarming around me. I knew that God had called me to preach, but what would be the outcome? I prayed and waited. I waited and prayed. My wife had prayer warriors praying nonstop. They were all lifting me before the throne of God, pleading for my life. Me? I was just asking God to speak. I was asking Him to save the souls of the men and women before me. I just wanted God to move. I *needed* God to move.

As I started preaching, the chief of police shouted, "At my signal, you shoot this man!" He was ordering his men to shoot me. For what? Murder? Theft? Adultery?

No. None of those things were the reason for my death sentence. The order had been given because I was preaching about Jesus. That's it.

I preached with a gun in my face for forty-five minutes.

As I began to preach, there was pin-drop silence. Everyone waited to see what the man with a gun to his head would say.

So what did I preach? I preached about the uniqueness of Jesus, about His wonder and perfection, and about the reasons for His awesomeness. I preached about why and how He is different from all the other gods and goddesses.

I preached with a gun in my face for forty-five minutes. By the end of the message, the chief of police came to me and said, "I have never heard about this Jesus. He sounds amazing. I think I could follow Him, too." Then he promised me that if I ever visited his area again to preach, he and his men would protect me.

Let me give you a little background on this story.

I was traveling to the Indian state of Punjab to preach in an area where the Gospel had never been publicly proclaimed. Can you believe that? There are still areas in the world that have never heard the name of Jesus. Today more people know the name of Osama bin Laden than the name of Jesus. More people in the world have tasted Pepsi and Coca-Cola than have heard the name of Jesus.

Before I got to Punjab, people apparently heard that I was coming. Riots were already breaking out. The Hindu extremists did not want anyone going to that area to preach about Jesus. They intended to do everything they could to stop me. As soon as I reached the city, the police met our vehicle and took us to the police station. On the police chief's desk was a paper that they wanted me to sign. It basically said, "I give you permission to shoot me if what I am about to say causes a riot in our city."

Seriously. This isn't made up. They wanted me to sign my name, giving the police written permission to kill me if my preaching caused any local problems. The man I was with grabbed the paper right away. "Sure! We'll sign. Where do I need to put my name?"

I said, "Of course, you'll sign, brother! You aren't the one preaching!"

After calling my wife and getting prayer warriors on their knees all over India, I signed the paper.

(Side note from Josh: Dr. Lall is too humble to put this in print, so I'll add this part. His friends also told him that they would have a car parked right behind the stage so that if anything happened, he could turn and run to the vehicle as fast as he could and avoid being shot. Dr. Lall's response was, "I will not get shot in the back for Jesus!" Is that a true Christian extremist, or what?)

Shortly after that event, a church was established in that same area. Not only that, but that same church planted a second church in a nearby village, and it continues to reproduce to this day.

That's what extreme boldness can do. It can spark a movement for the Kingdom of God that no man can stop. Remember what was written in the book of Acts? "If this is a move of God, then no one can stop it."

I'll say amen to that!

Have you noticed what people prayed for when difficulty rose up in the early church? They didn't pray that the difficulty would stop. They didn't pray that the persecution would end.

Take a look at their prayer in the book of Acts:

> *"'Now, Lord, consider their threats and enable your servants to speak Your word with great boldness. Stretch out Your hand to heal and perform signs and wonders through the name of Your Holy Servant, Jesus.'*
>
> *"After they prayed, the place where they were meeting was shaken. And they were all filled with the Holy Spirit and spoke the Word of God boldly."*
>
> —Acts 4:29-31

What does this boldness look like? To describe it, I will tell you about a friend of my father's who was an incredible preacher. His name was Jeevan Singh, and he was one of the boldest men I have ever known. He once told me a story that shook me to the core. He said that several years earlier, he had gone to a carnival in a small town in central India. There was a man at the carnival who practiced black magic, and he could do incredible things. He would amaze the crowd by performing different curses. This was no normal magician; his power came from the demonic world. He cut and placed a curse on a tree, and it withered and died. He could curse an animal, and it would not eat again. Local villagers would pay him to put curses on their enemies. He was the real deal.

On that day, he was showing off his powers. Hundreds of people were watching, astonished. He was able to place a curse on random people in the audience, and they began bleeding from their mouths and noses. People were fainting and falling over.

Jeevan Singh was watching all of this, and finally he had enough. He stood up in front of the crowd and offered a challenge to the witch doctor, "None of your curses can work on me. Jesus lives inside of me, and His power will protect me. He is much more powerful than all of this dark magic."

The crowd fell silent. They were shocked that someone would challenge this powerful sorcerer. At first, the magician laughed, but then he realized that Jeevan was serious. So he offered a challenge back, "Fine. I will accept your challenge on one condition—if I defeat you and your Jesus, you must serve me as a slave for the rest of your life!"

Jeevan immediately agreed. He knew that no power was greater than Jesus. Before the "spiritual competition," Jeevan prayed, "Jesus, show Your power here. By Your name and the power of Your blood, protect me from these evil attacks."

In front of hundreds of people, the man started "throwing" curses at this bold pastor. Nothing happened. He kept trying. Over and over and over again he tried. Still nothing. Finally, after every curse failed, Jeevan spoke, "See? Your power is useless against Jesus. I don't want to harm you. I just want to pray for you."

If Pastor Jeevan can challenge a witch doctor and show the power of Jesus, then imagine what you and I can do with a little boldness.

In front of the crowd, Jeevan and a few of his friends dropped to their knees and started praying against the demonic influence that was controlling this man and giving him power. The man started going crazy! He was screaming and jumping. He was beating his chest and cutting himself. After a few minutes of this, the demons left the man, and he fell to the ground. All of his power was gone.

That day, because of one man's bold stand, the entire crowd witnessed that the power of Jesus can conquer any evil. Then Jeevan began to share the Gospel with the magician, and after several months of meeting with him, the magician accepted Christ! He even became a leader in the local church.

If Pastor Jeevan can challenge a witch doctor and show the power of Jesus, then imagine what you and I can do with a little boldness.

Extreme Challenge

A. True boldness comes in many shapes and forms. It's an inner conviction to stand for the truth, regardless of the threat. That's not easy. It's difficult to go against the majority. If you stand alone, people will ridicule you and make fun of you. They will mock you and persecute you. Just remember: you're in good company. It has happened to many people throughout the centuries.

I think that to be bold, one needs practice. It doesn't just happen. The power behind boldness is the ability to face your fears. Take a moment now to list your top three fears. Of what are you truly afraid?

1. _____

2. _____

3. _____

To practice boldness in your life, decide now to take the first step toward bold Christian extremism. Face your fears! This will help your body to learn that it is your slave, not your master.

Within the next two weeks, make a plan to face your fears head-on. Are you afraid of heights? Go skydiving! Are you afraid of the dark? Spend a night outside under the stars. *All night.* (Is that too extreme?)

You may not think these are "Christian extremist" kinds of fears, and you would be right. But the truth is, sometimes you need to learn how to face your smaller fears before you can face your bigger ones. Sometimes you just need to build up your "boldness" muscles.

B.   Once you've done that, it's time for part two. List the names of five people you know who don't know Jesus.

1. _____

2. _____

3. _____

4. _____

5. _____

Pray for them every day. Then take them out for coffee. One by one. And share your faith with them. Scared to share? Face the fear. Be bold! You've already practiced facing smaller fears. Pray to the King of Kings, take a deep breath, and tell the people close to you how amazing Jesus is.

Now, watch to see what happens!

There is enough for everyone's need, but not enough for everyone's greed.

—Mahatma Gandhi

Chapter

The Spark of
Extreme Generosity

MY WIFE AND I (Josh) travel quite a bit in America when we are raising funds for our work in India. I remember one hotel where we stayed. We walked into our room, and everything was just plain wrong. Have you ever been to a hotel like that?

The bed was too hard. The paint color on the walls was too light. The carpet was old and nasty. The shower had no water pressure. The paintings on the walls looked like I drew them (and believe me, that's not good).

It was just bad. So we decided we couldn't stay in such horrid conditions. No other hotels were nearby, so we did what anyone would do in our situation. We went to a home improvement center and ordered new carpet. A few guys came to the room, tore up the old, nasty one and put in a new one. We went to a gallery and bought new paintings for the walls. A department store had an awesome shower head that promised better water pressure, so we bought it and promptly installed it. A furniture store supplied us with a new mattress, which was the most comfortable thing we had ever lain on. We even had a professional painter come in and change the wall colors.

It was the same room, but the atmosphere was completely different. It was as if we were on a reality show where they do a makeover of a house in twenty-four hours. It was awesome. *We stayed there for three days.*

Compared to the span of eternity, our life on earth is like a three-day hotel stay.

I'm sure you've caught on by now. We never did such a thing. If we did, all of the churches that aid us would promptly withdraw their support, right? It would be crazy if we really did such a thing, a complete waste of our time and money.

But are we that different in the way we spend our money? This world is not our home. Compared to the span of eternity, our life on earth is like a three-day hotel stay. Have you ever seen Francis Chan's rope illustration? He explains it like this: imagine that you have a rope that goes on and on forever. There is no end. Then take a piece of red tape that's a few inches long and cover the first few inches of the rope with the tape.

That tape represents our lives. It is nothing compared to eternity, but all we focus on are those few inches. Every second of every day, we focus on how we can make those few inches of tape the best ever. In the context of eternity, it just doesn't make sense.

Think about it. We are aliens, foreigners, sojourners, travelers, seekers, gypsies. We are traveling from one world to the next and trying to take as many people with us as we can. This reality should change the way we spend money. It should change the way we view our future, our retirement, our lives, and our marriages.

An eternal perspective will literally change the way we do *everything*.

Several years ago, I (Ajai) was preaching in Chhattisgarh, India. I was at a conference, and more than one hundred thousand people had gathered to hear the Gospel. It was truly a mountaintop experience. In seven days, I preached eighteen times.

My final sermon of the week was not to a large crowd. It was to a small leper village that my father-in-law, Dr. Henry, had founded many years before. He's the man we talked about earlier. At the end of the service, the local preacher announced to the crowd that they were going to take up an offering so that they could send a preacher to a nearby village to tell them about Jesus.

As I looked over the crowd, I saw an elderly woman walking to the front of the church. She was holding out her arms in front of her and had her hands pressed flatly together like she was praying. She had no fingers; leprosy had made sure of that. Pressed between her fingerless hands was a 100-rupee note, which is a little less than $2.00.

More than likely, that was all of the money she had. She was a leper, living in a leper colony, and she had no family members to take care of her. But there she was, giving everything she had so that the Gospel could be spread to the next village.

Are we truly being the stewards God has called us to be? What are we willing to give for the spread of the Gospel?

I broke down crying. I had thought that preaching to a massive crowd just a day earlier was my mountaintop experience, but the truth was that seeing this woman give all she had to the Kingdom was the true Mt. Everest. I felt like I had been transported to the temple in Jesus' day when an old widow had given a little mite, and Jesus praised her, saying that she had given more than anyone else because that was all she had.

If the widow in Jesus' day and the leper in our day could be so generous, then what is stopping you and me? Are we truly being the stewards God has called us to be? What are we willing to give for the spread of the Gospel? Are we too selfish to sacrifice our money for the sake of the global Kingdom? Where do our hearts lie?

Do you realize that $200 can support a preacher and his family in India for an entire month? And $30 per month can feed a hungry child, pay for his or her education, and provide the medical care that they desperately need? Sometimes I think that we don't realize how truly blessed we are and how easy it is to help others. We have not been blessed so that we can keep it all for ourselves. We have been blessed so that we can bless others in a massive way.

Think about it: eighty percent of the world is living on twenty percent of the world's resources, and twenty percent of the world is consuming eighty percent of the world's resources. That's like two kids at school having eight school lunches and eight kids having to share two lunches. It's not right.

Do you realize that if you make $40,000 per year, you are in the top 0.57 percent of people in the world? Just $40,000 per year! Most Americans say, "I can't even get by on that!" But we are the richest people in the world.

Using the same example salary ($40,000 per year), let's look at some stats that will blow your mind. In one hour, you make $20.83. In that same amount of time, the average worker in Indonesia makes thirty-nine cents. It would take the average laborer in Ghana 250 years to make $40,000. If you're thirsty, it takes you only one minute and forty-three seconds to make enough money to buy a Coke. In Zimbabwe, they work for more than an hour to get that same Coke. Your monthly income could pay the salary for 174 doctors in Kyrgyzstan.

Crazy, isn't it? Don't believe me? Go to www.globalrichlist. com and put in your annual salary. See how you compare.

Experts say that to provide the world with basic health care, food, and water, it would take close to $20 billion. Americans spend that much in one year *on ice cream*.

Unbelievable, right?

Our society is incredibly wealthy and often we don't even realize it. Although there are more poor people in America today than fifty years ago, we live in a culture that is still relatively well-to-do, compared to the rest of the world, so it's not surprising that we can be unaware of the greater need. But the greater need is there just the same. Why do we not respond as we ought?

Brought up in a culture in which all our needs are met, we take our luxuries for granted. We are warm and well fed, and we live in nice houses. We have a standard of living that is comfortable and a society that has a strong focus on accruing wealth. Some writers have said that materialism is the disease of our age. We certainly have a great many things—cars, properties, riches, and technological marvels of all kinds. It seems normal to us that we have all this. Almost everyone we meet has the same level of wealth. There's even preaching that encourages the accumulation of stuff. We have been blessed by God. We are an entitled people. According to Scripture though, we should go from this point of advantage to a place of submission—giving our wealth and resources to God. We should consider how He would want us to use these blessings He has given us. And that is where the disconnect in our lives and hearts occurs. *We really think it all belongs to us.*

This error in our hearts and minds leads us down a deadly path. It doesn't look deadly, but it is. We delight in our riches, and our lives are compromised. At first, we carefully give our ten percent, but in time it can become a grudging act. Our hearts have been ensnared. Instead of the path of submission, we choose to gather the blessing to ourselves first and give away what is leftover. Naturally, we start comparing ourselves to the other rich people around us, and we come to the conclusion that our stuff isn't good enough. So we think we need more…and more…and more. We think, "Well, I deserve this! I worked hard for this money. It's mine after all!"

> We have not been blessed so that we can spend everything on ourselves. We need our hearts changed so that we can view our resources from God's perspective.

Deuteronomy 8:17-18 says, "You may say to yourself, 'My power and the strength of my hands have produced this wealth for me.' But remember the Lord your God, for it is He who gives you the ability to produce wealth, and so confirms His covenant, which He swore to your ancestors, as it is today."

We have not been blessed so that we can spend everything on ourselves. We need our hearts changed so that we can view our resources from God's perspective. God has given us a great responsibility. Are we being good stewards of what He has so graciously bestowed upon us for the benefit of others? We need to think His thoughts in this area. We could be doing so much more.

An organization called Generous Giving says, "In America, the acquisition of wealth since the Second World War has far outpaced levels of giving. Christians are traditionally considered some of the most generous people on earth, and the amount of money we give to charities increases steadily each year; however, the amount given by Christians, by percentage, falls further and further behind levels of their acquired and accumulated wealth and prosperity."

Several years ago, David Barrett, founder and editor of the *World Christian Encyclopedia* and *World Christian Database*, wrote a report that came to these two conclusions:

1. Where there has been pain and suffering, people have sought after Jesus Christ.

2. But where there has been excessive prosperity, a large majority of people clench their fists against Him and compromise quietly.

Here's the question: are we more like the leper we talked about earlier who gave it all, or are we more like the barn builder whom Jesus taught about in Luke 12? Jesus told a parable about a man who had an amazing harvest. He had more grain than he ever thought possible. He said, "Wow! This is incredible! I don't even have enough room in my barns to hold all of this. I know what I'll do. I'll tear down my barns and build bigger ones. Then I can sit back, relax, and enjoy the rest of my life."

Then God said to him, "You fool! You're going to die tonight. Who will get all that you stored up for yourself?" Jesus' message to us is that this is how it will be for anyone who stores up things for himself but is not rich toward God.

Bigger barns. Fancier houses. Elaborate church buildings. Faster cars. Better phones. Wide-screen televisions. The latest fashions. More things. Bigger, better, faster. We just want more and more.

Are we living our lives in light of eternity, or are we living our lives for this earth?

Are you and I taking hold of the life that is "truly life"?

In 1 Timothy 6:17-19 (MSG), Paul tells Timothy, "Tell those rich in this world's wealth to quit being so full of themselves and so obsessed with money, which is here today and gone tomorrow. Tell them to go after God, who piles on all the riches we could ever manage—to do good, to be rich in helping others, to be extravagantly generous. If they do that, they'll build a treasury that will last, gaining life that is truly life."

Are you and I taking hold of the life that is "truly life"? The truth is that, compared to the rest of the world, we are incredibly rich— perhaps not in the average American's eyes but definitely in the eyes of most of the world.

Even in biblical times, people knew they should honor God's command to help others, but sometimes they weren't sure how to go about doing that. The answer, found in Isaiah 58:10–11 (MSG), was as true then as it is today: "If you are generous with the hungry and start giving yourselves to the down-and-out, your lives will begin to glow in the darkness, your shadowed lives will be bathed in sunlight. I will always show you where to go. I'll give you a full life in the emptiest of places—firm muscles, strong bones. You'll be like a well-watered garden, a gurgling spring that never runs dry."

> "Show me your spending habits over the last month, and I'll show you where your heart is."

It's time to open our eyes and truly become Christian extremists, not only by the way we love and serve but also by the way we give. This isn't a ploy to get money. We're not going to ask for a donation. This isn't about writing a check and easing your conscience. It's about a worldview. Jesus has called us to live with a mindset of service and giving. This is about developing a selfless lifestyle.

Do we truly believe that the way Jesus tells us to live is really the best way? Is that the life that Paul talks about? Is money our master, or is Jesus our master? I once heard an old saying: "Show me your spending habits over the last month, and I'll show you where your heart is."

That's basically a paraphrase of what Jesus said: "Where your treasure is, there will your heart be also" (Matthew 6:21 RSV).

Again, who's our master, God or money? Are we really living generous lives? What if you woke up every day and asked yourself, "What can I give to the world today? Who can I bless today?"

The best kind of giving is the kind no one knows about except you and God. Our good deeds should be motivated by a sincere desire to help others and glorify Him. Sometimes people are motivated to be generous because it puts them in a favorable light with others. This may not even be a conscious motivation, but public recognition should not be our goal. Matthew 6:1–2 says, "Be careful not to practice your righteousness in front of others to be seen by them. If you do, you will have no reward from your Father in heaven. So when you give to the needy, do not announce it with trumpets, as the hypocrites do in the synagogues and on the streets, to be honored by others. Truly I tell you, they have received their reward in full."

The point is that we need to return to true biblical giving. We need an infusion of Holy Spirit giving in our lives. We need to submit our hearts to His Lordship in this matter. We need Him to change the way we manage our wealth so that we accomplish His purposes on the earth.

Extreme Challenge

It is not my intention to tell you where you should give your money or what to do with it. What I am going to say is this: choose a ministry or a mission somewhere in the world that is serving the poorest of the poor and the unreached peoples of the world and start giving money to them.

Go and visit them. Instead of buying that new phone upgrade, give the money you would have used to plant a church in a Third World country. Look at your life and make careful decisions about your needs. Don't just think in terms of tithing ten percent. That's easy. How much can you really sacrifice for the sake of the Kingdom? When we are intentional with what we have been given, we can partner with God to do great things.

Pray about that. Ask God to direct your heart and then decide on an amount you would like to give this year. Make it big. Make it extreme. Raise money if you have to. Get other people involved.

Write down the amount of money you want to give away this year, and stick to it! Don't write down a number that is "do-able." Write down a number that is out of your comfort zone. Write down a number that will take faith. And watch how God provides! Be generous, and bless the world with the blessings you have been given.

$ _____

Now, do some research and choose the organization that you would like to support. To seal the deal, write them a letter promising the amount of money that you wrote on the line above. This will give you the extra incentive to push on when things get tough.

Write the name of the organization here:

_____

Let's get out of the ranks of the complacent, the comfortable, and the wasteful. As faithful stewards, let's do something huge together!

Darkness cannot drive out darkness. Only light can do that. Hate cannot drive out hate. Only love can do that.

—Martin Luther King, Jr.

"Your kingdom come, Your will be done, on earth as it is in heaven..."

—Jesus

Chapter

11

Bringing Heaven to Hell

PETER IS ONE of my favorite disciples. Maybe it's because he reminds me a lot of myself (Josh). Always talking too much. Always putting his foot in his mouth. This time, though, he finally got it right. Jesus asked his disciples a couple of questions. First he asked, "Who do people say that I am?"

The disciples replied, "Well, some say you are Elijah, and some say you are one of the prophets back from the dead."

Then Jesus asked the second question, the same question He asks all people at some point in their lives, "But who do *you* say I am?" (Mark 8:29 NLT)

Many of us live our entire lives based on what other people say about Jesus. Our parents, our friends, our pastors, our churches.

As usual, Peter speaks up above the other disciples. He blurts out what he thinks. He really doesn't have a filter. Do you know anyone like that?

Peter says, "Jesus, you're the Christ, the Son of the Living God."

Everyone is silent. This could be blasphemy if he isn't right. But Jesus says, "You're right, Peter! And it's on this rock that I will build my church, and the gates of hell will not prevail against it."

On what rock would the church be built? On the rock of Jesus Christ, the Son of God. But do you know what gets me most excited about this encounter? It's Jesus' last phrase. That's the phrase that keeps my heart pumping: "The gates of hell will not prevail against it."

I have heard people say something like this about this Scripture: "See! Satan will not win. When he comes against you, he won't defeat you, so don't worry. He will attack, but he won't prevail!" And that's all well and good, but that's really not Jesus' main point.

Jesus wasn't talking about the church playing defense; He was talking about how we are on the offense. The ball is in the church's hands. The church members are the ones charging the gates of hell. Gates aren't used to attack; they are used to defend.

I love what the church leader Neil Cole has to say about this passage:

There is no power on earth that is capable of stopping the church from accomplishing the mission given to her by Jesus...except her own lack of faith. It is not Satan or his minions that threaten our success. It is not any cult, philosophy or "ism" that is holding us back. No government or ideology of hate can stop the church. The *only* thing that can hold us back is our misplaced and weak faith.

Most of us are familiar with gates and likely have one at home. What are gates good for? Gates keep dogs in the yard and prowlers out. Gates are not offensive weapons; they are defensive. Police officers do not carry loaded gates. Terrorists do not hold hostages at gate-point. Dogs do not wear signs that say "Beware of gates!" Gates are not a threat. In Jesus understanding, we are the threat, and the enemy is running scared! Jesus sees the church on offense and Satan back on his heels on defense with his tail between his legs.

If we understood church the way Jesus described it, we would not be waiting for the world to come to us; we would be taking Jesus to the very gates of hell and setting captives free.[12]

So Jesus is really saying, "When you storm the castle of hell and you bring light into that dark place, they won't be able to stop you. The gates will be destroyed!" The church is on the offense not the defense.

That's the call of the Christian extremist—to bring light into darkness. To bring heaven into the places on earth that look like hell and storm the gates!

That's what Divas is trying to do in northeast India.

Several years ago his sister began to share the love of Christ with prostitutes and their children in the area's largest brothel. She invited him to come and see her ministry. When he went, he couldn't believe what he saw.

Children were being raised in the brothel. Their mothers were prostitutes, and the children lived in the same rooms in which the prostitution was taking place. These children were watching everything that happened there.

Not only that, but they weren't being fed. Many of them were forced into a tiny room all day long and given only a small packet of crackers and a little water. The room had no windows. In that small room they were forced to inhale gasoline fumes, which would calm the children down and cause their hunger pangs to go away.

It was truly hell on earth for those children. Divas called us and told us about it. My (Josh's) wife, Lashi, visited this place shortly after we heard the news. She took with her love, grace, food, candy, toys, and gifts. The kids' faces lit up. They had never seen such love. Heaven was truly coming to hell. The gates of hell were being ripped off their hinges, just with a few hugs, a few kisses, and lots of love.

Darkness flees at the first sign of light. Imagine what your light can do in the dark places in this world!

Every week, Divas's sister does the same thing with these children, and every week hell is being transformed. Not only that, but we've been able to save eleven children out of this situation. Their mothers have asked our local team to take care of the children so that they don't have to live in such a horrible situation anymore. They are now going to school, getting proper nourishment, and learning about the love of Jesus.

That's what happens when a Christian extremist comes to town. Hell's doors are blown off, and the Kingdom of heaven comes pouring in. Darkness flees at the first sign of light. Imagine what your light can do in the dark places in this world!

The sad thing is that there are people in the world who are not spreading light. They are spreading darkness. They are not spreading heavenly principles but hellish philosophies. Extremists across the world are spreading fear, worry, pain, death, and destruction. Are you willing to stand up against them? Are you willing to be a light in these dark places? Are you willing to charge the gates of hell?

There are gates of hell all over the world. Right now, a child in America is being beaten by his drunken father. He needs love and hope. He's waiting for you.

Right now, a young girl in Nepal is being kidnapped and forced into prostitution. She is waiting for the door of her cell to be knocked down. She needs to be rescued. She's waiting for you.

Right now, a teenage girl is walking to an abortion clinic because she has no other option. No one loves her, and no one cares. She needs your healing touch. She's waiting for you.

Right now, a college student is standing on a chair with a rope around his neck. The world is too much for him. He doesn't want to live anymore. He needs to know that he's not alone. He's waiting for you.

Hate cannot drive out hate. Only love can do that."

I could go on and on.

Each of these scenarios is where the gates of hell have put up shop. This is where the king of darkness is ruling and reigning, and you have the answer. Will you respond? Will you answer the call? Will you hear their cries? Will you take heaven into their hell? Will you bring light into their darkness?

As Martin Luther King, Jr., said, "Darkness cannot drive out darkness. Only light can do that. Hate cannot drive out hate. Only love can do that."

According to Jesus, you are the light of the world. Shine brightly. Make darkness flee. Light never runs from darkness; it expels it. Darkness cannot live where light shines brightly.

In India, there is a group of children whom the locals call "balai" which means "demon" in English. They are treated like they are cursed by the gods. They aren't allowed to go to school. They aren't allowed to get water from the village well. They aren't allowed to play with the other children. They are outcasts, destined to live life alone.

And what horrible sin did they commit? What kind of dishonor did they bring on their families? None. They were born with the upper part of their lips missing. It's called a cleft lip or a cleft palate. The villagers believe that these children committed horrible sins in their past lives, so the gods have cursed them with this deformity.

Oh, the lies that Satan tells. His gates are standing strong on this one. No one is willing to change their minds unless, of course, some Christian extremists show up. In this case, the Christian extremists are doctors. One little surgery changes everything. One little surgery changes the future of each of these children.

After the surgery to correct the cleft lip and palate, the locals don't look down on the children anymore. They are allowed to go to school and play with the other children. They are no longer called demons but little heavenly angels whose faces show the sign of God's redemptive love.

Hell doesn't stand a chance.

Anyone from any walk of life can use the gifts that God has given them to kick down the gates of hell.

We've witnessed this transformation year after year when the Life Enhancement Association for People (LEAP) team comes to our local hospital. Plastic surgeons, dentists, doctors, and nurses from all over America leave the comfort of their homes and spend a week at our mission in India doing surgeries from morning to evening.

They shine their light brightly, and darkness runs and hides. The hell that these children live in is busted open, and heaven pours in. You don't have to be a preacher to be an extremist. Anyone from any walk of life can use the gifts that God has given them to kick down the gates of hell.

What do you have to give?

I remember hearing Dr. Tony Campolo, a pastor, speaker, author, and sociologist, tell a story about his time in Haiti many years ago. He was going back to his hotel after a long day at the ministry where he was serving when a few young girls approached him. They were between ten and twelve-years-old, but they were dressed like they were twenty. They were prostitutes, and they were trying to get Tony to pay for their services.

He asked them, "How much? Seriously. How much for all three of you?"

They gave him a price.

He said, "I want you up in my room in thirty minutes."

He gave them his room number and walked away.

You may be thinking, "What? What is this preacher doing? Has he fallen into sin?"

Tony went up to the room and ordered cake, ice cream, soda, and candy. He asked the hotel staff to bring a DVD player and a television to his room with every Disney movie they could find. The three girls walked up to the room, thinking they would be raped by this man all night, but instead, they were met with a party. Disney movies and cake and ice cream!

They fell asleep late that night watching movies together. For one night, their hell was turned into heaven. For one night, they were safe. For one night, darkness no longer ruled. Light had come.

Extreme Challenge

Set this book down right now and take a moment to be silent before God. In your life and community, think about where the gates of hell have set up strongholds. Allow God to place areas and locations on your heart. Where are people suffering? Where are people hurting? Where are people without Jesus?

Write them down here:

_____

_____

_____

Now call a few friends together and make a plan. Pray for these places and decide together what you can do to bring the love of Jesus there.

Need some inspiration? How about Savannah Christian Church in Savannah, Georgia? Every week, a group of women from the church get together and take food to the local strip club. No men! Just women. They take the food to the dressing room, talk with the girls, feed them, love on them, and then leave. They are taking heaven into hell. They are only there for about thirty minutes, but week after week those thirty minutes make a huge impact!

This is just one example, but there are many ideas if you put your mind to it. Use your imagination. What is something practical that you and your friends can do in order to bust down the gates of hell in your neighborhood and shine light into the darkest places? Make a plan now and write it down here:

*It stands to reason, doesn't it,
that if the alive-and-present
God who raised Jesus from
the dead moves into your life,
he'll do the same thing in you
that he did in Jesus, bringing
you alive to himself? When
God lives and breathes in you
(and he does, as surely as he
did in Jesus), you are delivered
from that dead life. With his
Spirit living in you, your body
will be as alive as Christ's!*

—ROMANS 8:10-11 (MSG)

Chapter

Bringing Dead
Things to Life

I n EZEKIEL 37, Ezekiel has a vision that may give you night-
mares! God takes him to a valley that is filled with bones.

Not just any bones—human bones.

It's a massive graveyard, and the bones are of people who
have been dead a *long* time. There is no flesh left—just piles
and piles of dry bones.

God tells Ezekiel to speak to them.

Speak to bones?

Ezekiel obeys. He commands the bones to stand up and
come together, and they do, eventually.

> What God did in the valley of dry bones through Ezekiel, God can do in your own heart and life as well.

First, though, God commands Ezekiel to call for ligaments and muscle and flesh. He does so, and the bodies are complete again. All they need is the breath of life. So Ezekiel calls to the wind, and life fills the bodies once again. What was once a valley filled with dead, dry bones is now a valley filled with a massive, living army!

That's what Christian extremists do. They bring dead things back to life. Dead hearts, dead minds, dead marriages, dead families, dead passion. We serve a God of resurrection.

You may have started this book feeling dead inside. Maybe you lost your sense of life a long time ago. Maybe you desperately need to be revived. Here's the good news: what God did in the valley of dry bones through Ezekiel, God can do in your own heart and life as well. Dead things can't stay dead when Jesus is around.

Do you know where the most dangerous place in the world currently is? It's not Iraq or Afghanistan. It's not India or one of the many dangerous cities in South America. The most dangerous place in the world is inside a mother's womb.

More than forty million abortions happen every year. Abortion kills more people than anything else worldwide. Second to abortion is heart disease which kills close to eight million people every year, not even close to the abortion statistic.

Why am I telling you this in a chapter about bringing dead things to life? Because that's what our workers are laboring to do in India as they work with pregnant teens and attempt to curb abortions. Compared to the large numbers just quoted, the numbers at our mission may seem very small. But remember, every number is a human life. Every number is a baby boy and a baby girl with a life and a future.

Several years ago, our hospital began to fight against abortion. It's so common in India that when a woman goes to the doctor, one of the questions on the form is, "How many abortions have you had?" They aren't even asking if she has ever had one—they are asking *how many*. So we started a ministry to help teenage girls with their pregnancies.

Unwed pregnancy in India is a problem that brings shame to the entire family and village. A girl will do anything to save herself from this shame and dishonor—even kill the baby immediately after he or she is born. We have found babies in train toilets and in plastic bags on the sides of local roads. By the grace of God, some of them have been found alive, and we've been able to rescue them.

We set up a secret home in our city where young, pregnant girls can come and hide until their babies are born. No one knows their names, and no one knows where they come from.

We are saving babies from the clutches of death. In the past five years, through this ministry, we have already saved more than sixty children. The young mothers have placed them in the care of our children's home, which Josh's wife, Lashi, directs.

Our local people are truly practicing resurrection. Babies who had no hope and no voice are now getting another chance at life.

Sanjay Nayak was the only child of a village chief in the state of Chhattisgarh, India. He was basically the prince of their tribe. His family had been leading the tribe for generations, and because Sanjay was the only child, he was slated to take over as village chief when he got older. His family was from the highest caste Hindu tribe. They took care of the local temple and even performed animal sacrifices to the gods. Sanjay helped with all of this. He was being groomed to lead.

He studied in the local village school until the fifth grade. After that, his father sent him to the city for further study, an eight-hour trip away from their village. He wanted his son to have the best possible education so he would be able to lead their people well.

Things went fine up until the tenth grade. At that point, Sanjay became involved with drugs, alcohol, and the wrong crowd. As a drug dealer, he became incredibly wealthy, even in high school, but one day it all came crashing down. The police caught him with fifty pounds of marijuana and put him in prison.

After a few days, word got back to his father. His father drove the eight hours to bail his son out of prison and then drove him back to the village. Sanjay tried to speak to his father several times on the eight-hour journey home, but his father would not even look at him. He completely ignored him the entire time.

Sanjay knew he had brought great disrespect to his family, but he had no idea what his father was about to do. When they pulled up to their home, close to two thousand people were waiting for them. As Sanjay and his father walked in front of the crowd, Sanjay's father grabbed his son's hand and held it high into the air. Then he made a public declaration that would change Sanjay's life forever. "As you know, our family has served this village with peace and justice for many generations. My son has brought great dishonor on our entire village. Because of this, I now publicly declare that he is no longer my son. I disown him. He will not take over leadership after I am gone, he will not receive the inheritance of our family, and he will no longer be welcome in our home."

The father then threw his son's arm down, walked to a table, and signed a legal document that confirmed what he had just spoken. Without saying a word, the father turned his back on Sanjay and walked away.

Sanjay had been kicked out of his family and was no longer welcome in his village. Can you imagine what that must have been like? At the age of seventeen, he was publicly rejected by his entire family. So Sanjay did the only thing he thought he could do. He went back to the city to continue with his old gang.

Things got worse. He became involved with prostitutes, murderers, and heavy drugs. He did anything and everything imaginable. Because of this lifestyle, Sanjay kept getting in trouble. He was in and out of prison over and over again. After he was released for the fifth time, Sanjay had had enough. He couldn't go on anymore. Every day, his father's words haunted him. Every day, he felt the shame he had brought to his family. Every day, he felt dead and worthless. Every day, he wanted to end his life.

Sanjay finally decided that suicide was his only option. He went into the city on a Sunday afternoon, which is the day everyone goes to the local market. There was a large crowd in the marketplace. He walked into a shop and bought a bottle of poison that local people used to kill insects. His plan was to go back to the place where he stayed and drink the whole bottle. After buying it, he turned around and heard someone yelling in the middle of the marketplace. A crowd was forming. He was curious to see what was happening.

As he walked through the crowd, he saw a man talking about someone he had never heard of before—a man named Jesus. Sanjay had never heard this name before. As the preacher was speaking, he noticed Sanjay in the crowd. He had seen him before. As a matter of fact, he knew Sanjay's father.

After the preacher finished his sermon, he walked over to Sanjay and asked him what he was doing there. "You're the son of the village chief, aren't you? What are you doing way out here?"

Sanjay told him the whole story with all the gory details. He even confessed to the preacher that he was planning to take his life that afternoon.

The preacher had compassion on him and told Sanjay that he could come live with his family for a while. Sanjay accepted the invitation and stayed with the preacher for about a week. This is where the story really gets interesting.

I (Ajai) was traveling to that same area. The preacher who Sanjay was staying with had planned an open-air evangelism meeting and asked me to preach. I knew nothing about Sanjay, but he attended our first service with the preacher.

That night, I preached a sermon about the Prodigal Son. I had no idea that I was preaching to the prodigal son himself. But, unlike the young man in the Bible story, the prodigal village prince sitting in the crowd did not receive open arms when he went home. He received rejection. After hearing about the love and grace of the Father God and the way He forgave the Prodigal Son in the story, Sanjay came forward and accepted Jesus as His Lord.

God brings dead things to life. Sanjay was about to kill himself. He was dead inside, but God brought him back to life and filled him with love and hope. He revealed His grace to Sanjay. He lifted out the dead things in his heart and restored his life again.

Sanjay stayed with my wife, Indu, and I for six months and then went to Bible college to become a preacher. After graduation, Sanjay decided he wanted to start his ministry in the same area where he had been rejected five years before.

He went back to his home village to preach the Gospel. The prince who was rejected found acceptance in Christ and went back, not as a prince of the tribe but as a prince of the true King. He had been resurrected.

For two years, his parents acted like they didn't know him. They would not even look at him. For two years, Sanjay preached faithfully. He planted ten churches in the surrounding villages. Ten churches! God was using this resurrected man to bring life into the dead hearts all around him.

Finally, after two years of preaching, Sanjay's father sent word through a local villager that he wanted Sanjay to come back home but on one condition. He said, "I want Sanjay to bring with him the man who changed the demon-child into a saint."

> The hardest of hearts and the deadest of souls can be brought back to life again by the resurrection power of Jesus.

To fulfill his father's wishes, Sanjay knocked on my door. He and I both knew that I had not changed his heart; only Jesus could have done that, but he asked if I would go with him to see his family for the first time since he was disowned.

So I went. I stayed with Sanjay and his parents for a few days. They could not believe the transformation that had taken place in their son's life. It made such an impact on them that on the final day of my visit, they told me that they were ready to be baptized. As the prodigal son watched, I baptized the village chief in the name of Jesus.

There is no thing and no person who is too dead to be brought back to life by Christ. The hardest of hearts and the deadest of souls can be brought back to life again by the resurrection power of Jesus.

That's what Christian extremism is all about. It's about opening up our hearts and our lives so that God can use us to bring dead hearts and dead things back to life again.

Are there dead things in your life right now? Family members who have no hope? Friends who don't know Jesus?

Remember that valley of dry bones that Ezekiel saw? That is still the vision of God for all of us—that His Spirit would breathe on us and bring all of us back to life and that we would become a spiritual army who will bring life into the deadest places on earth.

That's the vision of a Christian extremist—to bring dead hearts back to life with the resurrection power of Jesus. Don't you want to see that kind of transformation? Don't you want to see that kind of miracle? Then what's stopping you? Allow God's Spirit to fill you with His love and grace, to bring the deadest parts of *your* heart back to life, and then to use you to take that same resurrection to everyone around you.

Lazarus, come out of your grave...

Extreme Challenge

Whom can you think of that is like Sanjay Nayak in your life? Is there someone you know who causes you to think, "There is no way that person will ever become a Christian"?

Take a moment to pray about that. Who in your life has the hardest heart?

Write his or her name here:

_____

Here's the challenge:

Make a commitment for the next forty days to pray for this person. Every day. Pray that God would bring his or her heart back from the grave. Pray that God would open their hearts and soften them to His love. After praying for forty days, reach out to them. Invite them out for coffee and share the love of Jesus with them. Let's watch as God brings dead hearts back to life all over the world!

He is no fool who gives
what he cannot keep to gain
what he cannot lose.

—JIM ELLIOTT

Chapter

The Spark of
Extreme Sacrifice

'M SURE THAT you've noticed by now a common thread that
runs through every trait of a Christian extremist: the willingness to sacrifice. Jesus Himself tells us to "pick up your cross
and follow Me."

He says, "No one who puts his hand to the plow and looks
back is worthy of following Me." Jesus was willing to sacrifice
everything for you and me. The question is this: what are we
willing to sacrifice for Him?

The apostles didn't shrink back when they were asked this
question. To them, no sacrifice was too great for the King of

Glory. They gave it all. They died with their boots on. They risked everything for the sake of the Gospel. When difficulty came, they didn't flinch. They stood firm and gave it all for the Man from Nazareth who was the Son of God.

Think about it: Matthew was killed in Ethiopia with a sword. Mark was dragged by horses in Egypt until he was dead. Luke was hanged to death in Greece. James the Just was thrown off of the top of a temple. A one-hundred-foot drop! This was the same place Jesus had been taken during His temptation. When they saw that the fall did not kill James, they beheaded him.

James the Greater, the brother of John, was beheaded in Jerusalem. Church history says that the guard who was assigned to James was so convicted by the words that James said at his trial that he also accepted Jesus and knelt down beside James to get beheaded with him.

Philip was crucified like his beloved Lord. Thomas was killed with a spear on the southern shores of India. Jude was killed with arrows when he refused to deny Jesus. Andrew was severely beaten and then crucified on an X-shaped cross in Greece. His followers said that when he saw the cross, he saluted it and said, "I have always longed for this happy hour. The cross has been consecrated by the body of Christ hanging on it." He hung there for two days and preached to those watching until his last breath.

Matthias was stoned and then beheaded. Bartholomew was whipped to death in Asia. Barnabas and Stephen were stoned to death. Peter was crucified upside down because he did not feel worthy to be crucified in the same way as Jesus. Paul was beheaded in Rome after many other trials that are recorded in the book of Acts. The only way they could get Paul to stop preaching was to cut off his head.

All but one of the early apostles sacrificed his life for the love of Christ—the apostle John. Tradition says he was boiled alive in oil but miraculously survived. Then he was sent to the island of Patmos as an exile. That's still sacrifice in my book.

> Christian extremists sacrifice every day for the sake of the Kingdom. They live for Christ; they die for Christ.

The band, Unspoken, wrote a song about this entitled, " Bury the Workman." (You can listen to it here: https://www.youtube.com/watch?v=VKw2TDCj0k0).

How can men stand like flint in the face of such pain and suffering? How can they sacrifice everything without turning back? The truth is, they didn't fear death. They all held the same philosophy as Paul: "For to me, to live is Christ and to die is gain" (Philippians 1:21). Hebrews 11:38 says that "the world was not worthy" of such men.

Christian extremists sacrifice every day for the sake of the Kingdom. They live for Christ; they die for Christ.

This is utterly different than extremists in other religions.

As I'm writing this, news is on the television of another suicide bomber attack in Afghanistan. It's January 29th, 2015. Apparently, a funeral was taking place for a police officer and a few others who were killed earlier. In the middle of the funeral, a man walked among the crowd and blew himself up, killing at least twelve people and injuring thirty-nine more.

All in the name of Allah.

This is extreme sacrifice at the opposite end of the spectrum. Some people sacrifice their lives to destroy. Others sacrifice their lives to save.

In Germany in the early 1700s, two young men named John Leonard Dober and David Nitschman heard the account of a former slave from an island in the West Indies. The slave said there were three thousand slaves working on the island who would want to be told about Jesus. None of them had ever heard of the love of Christ.

> "May the Lamb that was slain receive the full reward of His suffering!"

Both men were deeply convicted that these people would die without ever hearing about Jesus. So they created a plan. They decided to sell themselves into slavery so that they could reach the island and tell the slaves about Jesus. They were told they could not do this because they were white, but still they determined to get to the island and preach by some means. Their families and even their church were against this decision. David and Leonard were in their early twenties and had the rest of their lives ahead of them. Their friends and families pleaded with them not to go, but the young men wouldn't listen. Finally, they were allowed to go with the understanding that their primary function on the island would be to work, and they could preach on the side. John was a potter and David, a carpenter.

As the two men set sail, leaving Europe, possibly never to return, they yelled to their friends and family members who were still on the pier, "May the Lamb that was slain receive the full reward of His suffering!"

This is extreme sacrifice. These men did not love their lives. They loved Christ, and they wanted to do whatever it took to share Him with those three thousand slaves.

The outcome? Through the course of their time on that island and the surrounding islands, over 13,000 people were baptized. All of this happened because two men were willing to risk everything to share the Gospel with a few thousand slaves.

It reminds me of a quote by the late English Christian evangelist Leonard Ravenhill: "What are you living for that is worth Christ dying for?"

> Is the life you are currently living worth the death of Christ? Or are you living only for yourself?

Ask yourself that question. What are you currently living for that is worth Christ dying for? Why did Jesus die anyway? Why did He sacrifice everything for you and me? Paul answers that question in 2 Corinthians 5:14-15: "For Christ's love compels us, because we are convinced that one died for all, and therefore all died. And he died for all, that those who live should no longer live for themselves but for him who died for them and was raised again."

Why did Christ die? So that we would no longer live for ourselves but for Him. Is the life you are currently living worth the death of Christ? Or are you living only for yourself? Are you only living to build your own kingdom? Is your prayer, "May my kingdom come, my will be done"? Or is it all for Christ? Is it for the sake of His name? Are you sacrificing everything you have for the Gospel of Jesus? Are you building His Kingdom or your own?

Think back to David and Leonard. Some may ask, "Well, how long did they live? When did these two men die?"

The answer is simple. They died before they ever set sail from Europe. Not physically, of course, but in every other way. They died to their own desires and to their own dreams. They picked up their crosses and followed Jesus into the unknown. They did not shrink back. They weren't afraid of death. You see, death has a different definition for a believer.

There's an old poem that goes like this:

Can This Be Death?

To be released from fear and sorrow.
To be released from sickness and pain.
To be removed from Satan's influence.
To be removed from sins enslavement.
To be presented in God's presence.
To be accepted in the fullness of Christ.

Can this be death?

To experience complete fulfillment as I look upon
His face.
To feast upon His glory and the riches of His grace?
Can this be death?
With all that heaven offers,
Its joy that overflows,
Its peace that knows no measure,
Its victory forever more.

Can this be death?

No, this is not death.

This is life. Eternal life.

—Author Unknown

What's the difference between suicide bombers and "suicidal missionaries" who are willing to sell themselves into slavery knowing that they will die? Both are doing it in the name of their God. But only one is doing it for the good of others. What are you willing to sacrifice for the sake of the Kingdom?

If there are men and women across the world who are willing to blow themselves up in the name of their gods and goddesses, then what are you and I willing to do for the sake of Christ?

Extreme Challenge

Take a moment right now and think about what Jesus is calling you to give up for the sake of His Kingdom. Your money, your time, college, your family, your friends, your future?

Spend some time right now in silence. Don't be afraid. Allow God to speak to you. Be open and willing to obey whatever He asks you to do. How will you change your life so that what you are living for is truly worth Christ dying for?

As you hear the voice of God, take the time to write down what He says. What does He want you to sacrifice for His Kingdom?

*Our greatest fear should
not be of failure, but of
succeeding at things in life
that don't really matter.*

—Francis Chan

*Disciple making is not a call to
others to come to us to hear the
gospel, but a command for us to
go to others to share the gospel.*

—David Platt

*"Go make disciples of
all nations…"*

—Jesus

Chapter

Now What?

T HROUGH THE PAGES of this book, you have been challenged time and time again to pick up your cross and follow Jesus—to live the life of a Christian extremist. Before I show you how, I'd like to set the stage. The game of chess was invented in India, and there's an old story about the man who invented the game.

Apparently, a king at the time was incredibly sad because he had lost his son in a devastating battle. This king locked himself in a room and wouldn't come out. A young man by the name of Lahur Sessa created a new game and took it to the palace. The king came out to see the game and fell in love with it. The game was incredible. To honor this young genius, the king said to Lahur, "Ask for anything, and I will give it to you!"

The young man said, "All I ask for is that you place one grain of rice on the first square of the chess board, two grains on the second, four grains on the third, eight on the fourth, and so on, until you fill every square with rice!"

The king laughed. He was probably even a little offended. He thought this was an incredibly stupid request. What? Did the king not have plenty of rice? He called in one of his servants and told him to fulfill the young man's request. After *hours* of counting rice grains, the servant went back to the king and said that it was impossible to meet the man's request.

"What? What do you mean? That's ridiculous!"

"No, King, this man is smarter than we gave him credit for. When each square is multiplied by two grains of rice, by the end of the board, we would have to give this young man more rice than exists in the entire kingdom! We would need 18,446,744,073,709,551,615 grains of rice!"

Just to put that number into context, this mountain of rice would be larger than Mt. Everest! As a matter of fact, that's nearly one thousand times more rice than the entire world produced this year.

Do you realize how quickly we could change the world if we used this principle in our approach to serving God? Do you see how our seemingly small actions, done once, done twice, done as a group and multiplied through this principle would have the power to transform the earth? Do you realize how powerful and influential your life could become over time?

That's the power of exponential growth. That's the power of small beginnings. That's the power of planting seeds and watching them multiply. Most people are content to think in terms of addition. Not extremists. They believe in the power of multiplication. It's not that extremists have more power, more ability, or even more faith. The Bible says it doesn't take much faith. In fact, Jesus says faith as small as a mustard seed is enough to move mountains. Extremists see opportunity in terms of multiplication, not addition. They understand that God is perfectly capable and willing to work through them to bring about change. That's why we at CICM have chosen multiplication over addition.

Let's put this law into a Kingdom perspective. The current world population is a little more than seven billion people. There is *no way* to reach this number of people without multiplication.

If I were to tell you that we could reach the entire world's population with the Gospel in less than twenty years, would you believe me? I didn't think so.

You might be thinking, *Jesus came two thousand years ago, and we still haven't reached the world. How can we reach the world in less than twenty years?*

We haven't reached the world because we haven't been obedient to Jesus' final command, "Go and make disciples of all nations." If we are obedient, it can happen. If we put our faith in Jesus and keep our commitment to Him, it can happen.

Jesus was repeating God's first command to humanity, "Be fruitful and multiply." The Great Commission is a rewording of this original command: "Go and multiply." That's what He was really saying.

What if you were the only Christian on the planet?

Let me show you how this multiplication could work if we use the same principle Lahur used with the chessboard. Let's start with one person. Only one person.

You.

We'll start with you.

You're the first grain of rice on the chessboard. What if you were the only Christian on the planet? What if Jesus was depending completely on you to spread His name to the ends of the earth?

You might be thinking, what? How could I do that? I'm not a great preacher. I'm not Billy Graham. I'm not Peter or Paul.

How can you do this? Let's say you commit to making one disciple every six months. That's all. One in six months. Every six months, you would move into the next square on the chessboard. If you teach your disciple to do the same thing, then in the next six months, you would move up another square. You just went from 1 to 2 and then from 2 to 4 in one year's time.

Nothing huge yet, but if everyone keeps passing this on, let's see what can happen:

Year	Number of Disciples
1	4
2	16
3	64
4	256
5	1,024

That's more than one thousand people in five years. That's amazing! Let's continue:

6	4,096
7	16,384
8	65,536
9	262,144
10	1,048,576

That's more than one million disciples in ten years. You've started an enormous movement, and you're just ten squares up that chessboard. Do you know how many people you have personally reached in ten years? Twenty. That's all. Twenty. Two people a year for ten years. But since all of them are doing the same work you are doing—together, you have reached one million people! Let's continue:

11	4,194,304
12	16,777,216
13	67,108,864
14	268,435,456
15	1,073,741,824

(For the record, that's almost the population of India. You and your disciples have reached India in fifteen years. Congratulations!)

| 16 | 4,294,967,296 |
| 17 | 17,179,869,184 |

If you make this commitment to make disciples and teach other people how to do the same thing, we can see our nation and the entire world transformed in less than twenty years.

Look at that number. That's almost three times the current world population. Do you know what that means? It means that in just a little more than sixteen years, you and your disciples have reached the entire world for Christ.

That's the power of multiplication played out in the Kingdom. If you make this commitment to make disciples and teach other people how to do the same thing, we can see our nation and the entire world transformed in less than twenty years.

Will you be the generation that will do this? Will you be one of the people who turns the world upside down? Will you be like Peter and Paul? Will you be one of the Christian extremists who takes the love of Jesus across the globe?

Before we get too far, we must first ask a question. It's probably one of the most important questions we can ask ourselves as followers of Jesus.

Am I a disciple that is worth reproducing?

In other words, am I following Jesus in a way that would inspire other people to follow Jesus whole-heartedly? Like Paul, can we say, "Follow me as I follow Christ?"

In this same vein, someone once asked me a question that rocked my world. "Josh," they asked, "If all Christians all over the planet lived like you live, what kind of church would we have? What would the Kingdom of God look like?" That question cut me to the heart because, the truth was, that the church would not look good at all if every Christian lived like me. It was a huge wake up call for me that I needed to begin to live differently. I needed to truly follow Jesus with all of my heart.

What about you? Let me ask you that same question: If every Christian across the world lived as you live, what would the world look like? Are you truly a disciple of Jesus whose life is worth multiplying all over the world? If not, then we must begin there. And that's what this book has been about. Start by putting these principles into practice. Start by living out extreme obedience and extreme prayer. Begin to use extreme boldness and extreme commitment. Live out all of the extreme challenges. Follow Jesus with all you have and be a disciple who is worth reproducing.

Then, exponential growth can happen through you. Our lives will reflect our relationship with Jesus clearly. Our focus in making disciples will guide us in our choices about how we use our time, our money, and our energy. We will walk in the strength of the Lord and make a massive impact in this world.

We will make disciples who make disciples who make disciples.

We believe in you. You can do this. Let's commit to this together. To help you, we are going to give everyone who reads this book a free fifty-two-week plan to guide you through the process of sparking this movement for the Kingdom of God—a Christian extremist field guide. Once a week, you will have a new mission sent to your inbox—a mission that will stretch you and guide you as you begin to make your sacrifice to change the world. We are also establishing an online community that will help you through the entire process. You can sign up at:

www.christian-extremism.com

We will be praying for you as you do this. Together we will live out these principles on a daily basis. Together we will start a movement that changes the world. As we lock arms with other people, more extremists like ourselves will be born. We will make disciples who make disciples who make disciples. Jesus said, "My true disciples produce much fruit. This brings great glory to my Father" (John 15:8 NLT).

May God be glorified through us as we lay down our lives for our friends and answer the call to Christian Extremism that

Jesus Himself modeled. Now together, let's be disciples that are worth reproducing. Let's spread His forgiveness and grace all over the world. Let's ignite the world with the love of Jesus. Let's start a movement. Let's become Christian Extremists.

Endnotes

1. "About Global Hunger," Bread for the World website, http://www.bread.org/hunger/global/.

2. "Micronutrient Deficiencies," World Health Organization website, http://www.who.int/nutrition/topics/vad/en/.

3. "ILO Says Forced Labour Generates Annual Profits of US $150 Billion," International Labour Organization website, last updated May 20, 2014, http://www.ilo.org/global/about-the-ilo/newsroom/news/WCMS_243201/lang—en/index.htm.

4. "Human Trafficking: Time for Change," Citizens for Global Solutions website, last updated October 8, 2014, http://globalsolutions.org/blog/2014/10/Human-Trafficking-Time-Change#.VOfukPnF9K8.

5. The Covering House website, http://thecoveringhouse.org/act/resources-2/sex-trafficking-statistics-source-documentation/.

6. Kiran Nazish, "Women and Girls, a Commodity: Human Trafficking in Nepal," *The Diplomat* website, last updated February 22, 2014, http://thediplomat.com/2014/02/women-and-girls-a-commodity-human-trafficking-in-nepal/.

7. "Violent Crimes against Children," Federal Bureau of Investigation website, http://www.fbi.gov/about-us/investigate/vc_majorthefts/cac/overview-and-history.

8. Tonny Onyulo, "Cornered But Still Defiant, Warlord Joseph Kony Eludes Capture in Uganda," *The Washington Times* website, last updated December 31, 2014, http://www.washingtontimes.com/news/2014/dec/31/joseph-kony-lords-resistance-army-warlord-eludes-c/?page=all.

9. "All about Life," Shot at Vaccines website, http://shotatlife.org/assets/downloadables/shot-life_allaboutvaccinesapril2012final.pdf.

10. "The Challenge," Global Opportunities for Christ website, http://www.goforchrist.org/the_challenge.

11. Disciple All Nations website, last updated February 28, 2014, https://discipleallnations.wordpress.com/2014/02/28/how-many-people-die-each-day-without-hearing-the-gospel/.

12. Neil Cole, *Cole Slaw*, "Jesus' View of Church," Posted March 1, 2015. http://cole-slaw.blogspot.in/2015/03/jesus-view-of-church.html.

Be a Match.
Spark a Movement.
Ignite the World.

Let us help you start Kingdom movements all over the globe.

- Visit ignitetheworld.co.

- Tell your church, group or organization about the Ignite eCourse, a step by step guide on how to spark a movement in your area that can change the world.

- Learn more about one-on-one Ignite Coaching to help start your movement.

- Read the Ignite Blog to learn more and get involved.

- Sign up for the Ignite newsletter via ignitetheworld.co.

It Only Takes One!

Serving Christ from the Heart of India

Founded in 1982 by Drs. Ajai and Indu Lall, Central India Christian Mission (CICM) has planted over 1,400 churches, secured sponsorship for over 5,000 children, trained over 450 Christian leaders, given medical treatment to over 60,000 people, and baptized over 400,000 people.

What started with two faithful servants has grown into a multifaceted mission reaching the unreached in and around India. Join the movement by:

- Visiting indiamission.org to learn more

- Telling your friends, family, church and small group about CICM

- Leading your church, small group or circle of friends in a fundraiser for CICM

- Sharing CICM's posts on Facebook Signing up for CICM's e-newsletters via indiamission.org

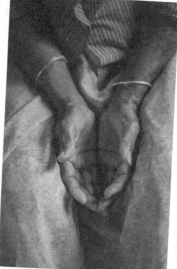

If you're a fan of this book, please tell others...

- Write about *Christian Extremism* on your blog, Facebook and Twitter.

- Suggest the book to your friends, neighbors and family.

- When you're in a bookstore, ask them if they carry the book. This book is available through all major distributors, so any bookstore that does not have this book can easily stock it!

- Write a positive review of *Christian Extremism* on www.amazon.com.

- Purchase additional copies to give away as gifts.

Connect with us...

To order another copy and or learn more about Central India Christian Mission , go to indiamission.org